FROM PAPYRUS TO PRINT

EARLY CHAPTERS IN THE HISTORY OF THE BOOK

KEVIN SPEARS

Published by Samizdat Books

All papers used are natural, recyclable products made from wood grown in well managed forests. The manufacturing processes conform to the environmental regulations of the country of origin.

British Library Cataloguing in Publication Data

Spears, K

From Papyrus to Print

A CIP catalogue record for this book
may be obtained from the British Library

ISBN-13: 978-1-90662-1995

Designed and typeset in Glastonbury and Lisbon.

Printed in Scotland by Bell and Bain Ltd.

Samizdat Books
Glastonbury & Lisbon
8A Market Place
Glastonbury, UK

For my grandsons, Justin and Adrian

Acknowledgements

David Thomas FBA, Emeritus Professor of Christianity and Islam, University of Birmingham, for his advice on improving Chapter 4.

Alastair Barr and Richard Kilroy for reading through a draft text and suggesting improvements.

Jim Woodcock for taking the cover photograph and the Chapter of Wells Cathedral for permission to reproduce it without charge.

Bernard Chandler for making the maps.

Gareth Mills for having the courage to take on publishing the book and for his friendship over some 20 years.

Stephen Parsons for his design skills in turning my draft into a readable book and for his patience in dealing with last minute corrections.

My wife, Lindsey, for her encouragement and forbearance as more and more books arrived in the post to aid my research, and for suggesting improvements to draft chapters.

CONTENTS

SURVIVAL OF GREEK LITERATURE

ARAL SEA

CASPIAN SEA

BLACK SEA

To BALKH

KHURASAN

• Constantinople

• Nisibis

• Edessa

To MERV
BUKHARA
SAMARKAND

• Antioch

• Baghdad

• Gondishipur

Basra •

PERSIAN GULF

SEA

• Damascus

• Jerusalem

• Alexandria

Cairo •

ARABIAN
DESERT

To MECCA
MEDINA

RED SEA

Map drawn by BernChandler@graffik.co.uk

SURVIVAL OF
ROMAN
LITERATURE

Map drawn by BernChandler@graffik.co.uk

PREFACE

This book has been written back to front. Three years ago I compiled a descriptive bibliography of the 115 books printed before 1555 belonging to the library of Wells Cathedral. Attached to the bibliography was an essay on the scholar printers responsible for their publication, and a second essay on the problems faced by these early printers. Modified versions of these two essays now form Chapters 7 and 8 of this book.

At the end of my work on the bibliography, I was aware that these early humanist printers were motivated to ensure that the new technology of printing would produce sufficient copies of the Greek and Roman classical writers so that their work would never be "lost" again, as it had been for almost 1,000 years through what is known as the Dark Ages. That raised the question as to what had been lost and why; and then, how what remained had been recovered?

At that time I could not find a book that gave me the answers. Which is why I started researching the subject and making notes. The research has been fascinating. I never knew that educated Romans were bilingual in Greek and Latin and were mostly taught in Greek; or that the Irish had founded so many monasteries in Europe which helped to preserve the Latin classics; nor was I aware of the role of the Arabs over a thousand years ago in translating and so preserving Greek scientific writing; that the Twelfth Century Renaissance was about rediscovering Greek scientific and philosophical works, whilst it was only in the later Italian Renaissance that the Greek literary inheritance found its way back to western Europe.

My notes have been turned into the earlier chapters in this book, and they lead on to the accounts of the first century of printing. Since I started my research, Violet Moller's entertaining book *The Map of Knowledge* was published in 2019. It does cover much of the same ground, but differs from mine as she tackles the subject through the history of science. My account has a focus on the history of the book, primarily through the role of the book trade and libraries, with more to say on the early printers. And it covers Roman literature as, unlike the Greeks, the Romans did not really "do" science.

I

INTRODUCTION

BOOKS IN ANCIENT GREECE AND ROME

Were it not for books, human culture would pass in to oblivion as quickly as man himself. **Pliny the Elder**

This chapter will look at how books were made and circulated in ancient Greece and Rome. A brief look at the history and environment of the period might be helpful:

Greek civilisation

It has not been clear to historians why the inhabitants of Greece launched an intellectual quest in the sixth century BC, the like of which had never been seen before, and which has guided western thinking for over two millennia since. And, unusually for the time, it was a secular outpouring of ideas and thought which covered philosophy, politics, science, mathematics and medicine. Writers have suggested several contributing factors: the political freedom and democratic form of government; the high level of literacy and debate; and the numerous contacts brought by colonisation into areas influenced by previous Egyptian and Mesopotamian civilisations.

Greek literature really began with Homer (c.850 BC), which is about the time the Greeks adapted the Phoenician alphabet to make writing easier. However, the *Iliad* and the *Odyssey* were oral compositions. They form the central works of ancient Greek literature, and it is thought that these works were first written down in the sixth century BC. These epic poems about gods with very human characters continued to be recited rather than read so that very few copies would have been made.

In the **Hellenic** period, from 750-323 BC, Greeks lived in hundreds of city states, or polis, of which Athens became the most important after the defeat of the Persians in 479 BC. These poleis mostly had populations of only a few thousands, with Athens reaching perhaps 250,000, about a third of whom were slaves. They were self-governing communities not dependent on gods, priests or kings unlike the earlier civilisations of the Minoans, Myceneans, Hebrews or Egyptians. And this lack of a hereditary, privileged, priestly caste with written scriptures and a vested interest in the status quo, gave the Greek intellectuals a comparative freedom.

The Greek philosophers understood that many natural phenomena had physical explanations rather than religious ones. Anaximenes (586-526 BC) realised that rainbows were caused by the sun's rays passing through dense air and not by the goddess Iris appearing. Pythagoras (c.570-495 BC) introduced logic saying that the mind and not the senses could find truth. Whereas myths are accepted unconditionally on faith and authority, the Greeks preferred systematic observation, logical proof, reason, and the critical analysis of theories. Theoretical thinking and systematisation of knowledge accompanied observation and collection of data. Hippocrates (c.460-c370 BC) was the first to realise that diseases had been regarded as sacred acts simply because of a lack of understanding. Astronomy became subject to geometrical explanation.

Citizens in the individual poleis actively participated and belonged to their cultural and political life. Laws were defined by man rather than divine rulers. Religion became largely ceremonial. Democracy was at its height by 450 BC.

It is in this Hellenic period, especially the fifth and fourth centuries BC, that all the familiar names of Greek philosophy (Socrates, Plato, Aristotle); the philosophical schools of Sophists, Cynics, Sceptics, Hedonists and Epicureans; the dramatists (Aristophanes, Euripides, Pindar, Aeschylus, Sophocles); the historians (Thucydides, Herodotus, Xenophon); and assorted literary figures from Aesop to Sappho were active. The advances in artistic expression, written history, medicine and science, philosophy, politics, lyric poetry, comedy and tragedy, have affected western civilisation ever since. Pericles in his famous funeral oration of 431 BC, honouring the dead of the Peloponnesian Wars, said: *Mighty indeed are the marks and monuments of our empire which we have left. Future ages will wonder at us, the present age wonders now.*

The **Hellenistic** period begins with the death of Alexander the Great in 323 BC and continues until the Roman conquest in 30 BC. Alexander's conquests to the east through Persia, Iraq, Egypt and across to north India via Afghanistan broke the mould of the city states and Greece became far more cosmopolitan. Shifting the capital to Egypt, with the founding of the city of Alexandria in 331 BC, helped move Greek culture away from its literary roots and the more limited cultural horizons of the poleis. Guided by Aristotle (384-322 BC), who had been the tutor of Alexander the Great, the earlier philosophy of Socrates and Plato gave way to natural philosophy based on reason alone, with the emphasis on astronomy, medicine, and mathematics.

The book trade in Ancient Greece

Hellenic Greece was essentially an oral culture and book production was limited. Plato (c.428-348 BC) had warned against the written

3

word as it circulated beyond the author's control, and so ideas could be misunderstood or misused more than when spoken directly to an interlocutor. Despite this prejudice against the written word, literacy was relatively high. It has been estimated that about 50% of the male population in the cities could read and write, and in Athens this would be nearer 100%. The comparative lack of cohesion between the city states meant that local dialects prevented a uniform version of the Greek language developing: Attic Greek was spoken in Athens, but Doric in Sparta and western Greece.

It was in the middle of the 5th century BC that we become aware that commercial books were circulating in ancient Greece. Socrates (470-399 BC) says that copies of the works of the philosopher Anaxagoras are available everywhere to buy for a drachma. The disdain that Socrates had for books was partly that the Sophists, especially Protagoras, charged money for their lectures and were obliged to provide students with books. Socrates was giving his lectures without charge and thought that was the way it should be. Authors would "publish" their work by making public readings. After the readings, students or copyists would write out as best they could from memory what had been said and these would then circulate. Eventually, "booksellers", people who would employ a team of copyists, would make additional copies for sale. Such books were written on papyrus rolls which will be discussed in the next chapter.

Practically nothing is known about the detailed workings of the book trade in ancient Greece. We do not know if authors received payment for their work and on what basis. There was certainly no copyright system and plagiarism was common.

Books would have been expensive and it was the rich who collected them. Papyrus had to be imported from Egypt. Educated slaves to make copies were rare, but Euripides was fortunate to have such a person which enabled him to build a library although not a wealthy man. The quality of scribes varied greatly. As demand for books grew, especially with the conquest of Greece by the Romans who became avid collectors, the quality deteriorated. Good slave scribes were expensive to buy, and so owners encouraged speed of production to maximise profit from their investment and this inevitably led to errors in their work. Lucian (c. AD125-180) was particularly scathing, and by his time even the Athenian booksellers had grown sloppy in maintaining standards, but were still regarded more highly than those in Rome or Alexandria.

In **Hellenistic** times, the period after the death of Alexander the Great in 323 BC, books circulated more widely. Alexandria became the centre of the book trade, in part as it was the source of papyrus. The papyrus fragments found in town rubbish tips of Graeco-Roman Egypt indicate books could be found on popular subjects such as cookery, angling, and horse breeding. The famous find in Oxyrhynchus (a once prosperous town 100 miles southwest of Cairo) turned up boxes of fragments that are mainly official and archival, but include 10% literary papyri ranging from Homer to Euclid and also early Christian texts. The fragments show that the second and third centuries AD were very active in book circulation with Homer, Demosthenes, Plato, Euripides and Menander being the popular authors. Mathematical and scientific books would always have been scarce compared with literary texts. After that, there is a considerable falling off as the Roman empire declined, and the number of Christian texts increased at the expense of the Greek and Roman pagan writers.

No specimens of early writing have survived from Greece. This may seem odd as we have writing from earlier civilisations such as the Sumerians, Babylonians, Hittites and Cretans. However, they used baked clay tablets which survive well. The Greeks used papyrus and occasionally animal skin. These do not survive in the Greek climate and soil unlike in the dryness of Egypt which is the home of papyrus.

Were there public or private libraries?

Private libraries were something of a curiosity at first in Athens. We have references to book collectors like Euripides from the fun poked at him by Aristophanes. We know of the private libraries of Pisistratus and Polycrates of Samos. These libraries would have been small and almost entirely comprised works of poetry. Unlike the Romans with their villas, Greeks led a more public, outdoor way of life and large homes with space for libraries were uncommon. There are no letters surviving that might have told us more about private libraries; the knowledge of Roman libraries was greatly helped by letters of Cicero and Pliny the Younger. No public libraries are thought to have existed before 527 BC which is when Pisistratus died and left his collection to the city of Athens.

Aristotle had a private library which would have been quite extensive to enable him to make his great compilations. He had founded the Lyceum in Athens to rival the Academy founded by Plato in 383 BC. Both of these scholarly institutions had libraries and it is said that the Lyceum had 2,000 students at a time. It is probably the earliest example of a living community of scholars, researchers, students and books that formed a great research library. Aristotle set an example to two of his disciples, Theophrastus and Menon, and it is not unreasonable to say that with Aristotle the Greek world passed from an oral culture to a written one. The foundation of the Library of Alexandria has a direct link back to Aristotle, not the least being that Aristotle was the tutor to Alexander the Great, but many think he may have been instrumental in the concept of a library that encompassed all the world's knowledge.

The Library of Alexandria

The date of the founding of this famous library remains uncertain. One claim is that Demetrius of Phaleron was tasked with its founding by Ptolemy I Soter who lived between 367-283 BC. Demetrius was a scholar who had compiled Aesop's fables and had been a student of

Theophrastus, a friend and student of Aristotle. Others think it was later and at the commission of Ptolemy II (283-246 BC). Ptolemy III created a secondary, smaller library known as the Serapeum as it was part of the temple of Serapis.

Ptolemy I was a Greek general who took over the Egyptian part of Alexander the Great's empire after his death and declared himself king, or pharaoh, of Egypt in 304 BC. The Egyptian third of Alexander's empire was in many ways the richest having the most fertile soils and agriculture with the bonus of ready access to papyrus. The Ptolemies were all intellectuals and they decided to distinguish Alexandria by making it a cultural centre. In order to attract the best minds to their capital, they built a research centre and the largest library in the world. This was also a way of asserting Greek culture in a foreign land with a recognised ancient civilisation of its own.

The library was combined with what we would call a research institute called the Museion, or Institute of the Muses, patterned on the Lyceum and Academy in Athens. These buildings formed part of the royal palace complex. At any one time some 1,000 scholars would work there, with their board and lodging paid for, including their servants, funded entirely by royal patronage. Research conducted was wide-ranging including all of the sciences and the literary heritage of Greece. It was here that the canon of Greek literature as we know it was defined. Manuscripts were collected from all over the world and scholars then decided the correct form of Homer and the early lyric poets by standardising the text and the format. They also wrote commentaries on the works of Greek literature.

Contents and organisation

The library's ambition was to collect all known written works and to become the memory of the world. Officials were despatched to acquire examples throughout the territories Greece had occupied and beyond. All the contents would have been papyrus rolls.

Inevitably there were duplicates, and some rolls contained more than one text. Estimates of the total stock at the end of the first century BC range from 400,000 to 700,000 rolls, which some have estimated to be about 100,000 modern books. Although the figure seems enormous, the library at Pergamon, which Mark Antony is said to have offered to Cleopatra, contained 200,000 rolls and so it is not an unrealistic figure.

The first director of the library was Zenodotus of Ephesus who was a Homer specialist. One of the library's scholars, Callimachus of Cyrene, devised a classification system assigning subjects to different areas. The eight subject groupings were: drama, oratory, lyric poetry, law, medicine, history, philosophy, and miscellaneous. Within their subjects, books were arranged alphabetically by author; the first known use of this system. Each papyrus roll had a tag attached with the author, title and subject of the work. Callimachus produced the *Pinakes*, the first library catalogue (now lost except for fragments). This catalogue filled 120 volumes and has the full title of *Tables of Persons Eminent in Every Branch of Learning Together With a List of Their Writing*. It amounted to a shelf list of the library but also carried a brief biographical note on each author.

Alphabetical order has been used ever since. Perhaps the most extreme example is noted in Manguel (1996) who tells of a tenth century Grand Vizier of Persia, Abdul Kassem Ismael, who travelled with all 117,000 volumes of his library. These were carried by a caravan of 400 camels trained to walk in alphabetical order.

Greek Scholars

The librarians themselves were scholars. Zenodotus was a grammarian and literary critic and it was he who first began the critical editing of Homer's epic poems. (Interestingly, papyrus fragments analysed from around towns and villages in Egypt would indicate that the *Iliad* was overwhelmingly more popular than the *Odyssey*). Eratosthenes was a polymath who measured the circumference of the earth and is now known as a geographer. Later directors, Aristophanes of Byzantium and Aristarchus, took the Museum back to literature and language. They furthered the work on Homer by writing commentaries and a lexicographical companion.

These scholars also produced what is known as the *Alexandrian Canon*: a list of Greek authors whose work was deemed worthy of preservation as classics. The list comprised 5 epic poets; 5 iambic poets; 9 lyric poets; 14 tragic poets; 13 comic poets; 7 poets of the Pleiades group; 8 historians; 10 orators; and 5 philosophers. The scholars then edited the surviving manuscripts by these writers to produce the authoritative versions that we know today. It was this editing that divided works into "books", for example, the 24 books of the *Iliad* and *Odyssey.*

In addition, Euclid studied at Alexandria as did Archimedes, Galen and Claudius Ptolemy. **Euclid** wrote the *Elements* here, and he did this by consulting earlier works of mathematics and then synthesising them with his own thinking. **Galen** went to search for the earliest medical and pharmacological manuscripts as these would have been regarded as more accurate. **Archimedes** did much of his work in his native Syracuse, but he spent time studying in Alexandria. As well as his mathematical writing, he was a great inventor known for pulleys, pumps, military catapults and even using metal mirrors to focus sunlight on Roman boats made of wood and setting them on fire.

Claudius Ptolemy wrote the *Almagest* which described the heavens and celestial bodies. From that work was abstracted the *Zij*, the most complete star catalogue of the ancient world which identified 1,022 of the brightest stars grouped in 48 constellations. The *zij* incorporated a table of mathematical formulae for calculating celestial positions. This revolutionised astrology and astronomy as, using an astrolabe, they could be adapted anywhere in the world to allow calculation of the position of the sun, moon, planets and stars. This work was to guide astronomers for over 1,000 years until the heliocentric model of Copernicus was adopted in the early sixteenth century.

The Greeks had defined the fundamental problems of the nature of matter, the structure of the cosmos, the nature of life, and studied them in rational, secular terms through observation, measurement and deduction. The recognition that nature operates through ordered systems, together with a mathematical language by which to describe them, is one of the lasting legacies of the Classical world.

The Ptolemies also ordered translations from other languages, including Egyptian. It was here in about 285 BC that 72 Jewish scholars translated the Old Testament from Hebrew into Greek to create the *Septuagint*.

What happened to the Library of Alexandria?

The fate of the Library of Alexandria is a bit like a murder mystery. There are several possible explanations of how it came to an end. Roman forces occupied Egypt in 30 BC but the emperors were content to see the library continue. Parts of it may have been destroyed by fire in 48 BC when Julius Caesar, having been attacked by an Alexandrian mob, burned boats in the harbour and the fire is said to have got out of control. The Roman Emperor Aurelian quelled a rebellion in Alexandria in AD 270 during which he destroyed much of the palace area and possibly what was left of the library. The Christian bishop of Alexandria was responsible for destroying the Serapeum in AD391 in order to rid the city of pagan works. In the destruction, the mob murdered Hypatia, who was one of the world's first female scientists and the daughter of the Serapeum's director, the mathematician Theon. In AD641 the Arabs invaded Alexandria and Caliph Omar is said to have ordered the destruction of all books that were not in accord with the Qu'ran.

However, the most likely explanation is that after the Romans took over and towards the end of their empire, money and motivation to keep up the endless copying of papyrus to preserve the contents was simply not there. In any case, by then the Ancient Greek language was unfamiliar and probably incomprehensible to the Alexandrians who were more likely to be users of Latin, Coptic, Aramaic, Hebrew, or Koine, the everyday local Greek language. Christian writing had also become more important, and Rome and Constantinople were now the intellectual centres. In all probability, the library just rotted away due to neglect and decay.

What did the Romans add?

According to Henry Chadwick (Boardman, 1989), *"The Romans, from Cicero to Pope Gregory the Great, regarded the Greeks as too clever to be honest. The Greeks, as is clear from Plutarch, admired the Romans, but did not greatly appreciate being conquered by them and would have preferred their own incompetent government to Roman efficiency and justice."*

When Rome conquered Corinth in 146 BC, Greece was absorbed into the Roman empire. The Roman poet Horace pointed out, however, that while Rome conquered Greece militarily and politically, the artistic and intellectual conquest belonged to the Greeks. Roman literature was slow to develop given the riches available to them from their new colony, and in its early stages there was a tendency to adapt or plagiarise Greek literature, especially the plays.

Roman literature dates from about 250 BC. In its earliest form it was unlike the epic poems of the Greeks and took the form of historical narratives. But exposure to the Greek classics through Mediterranean commerce, Greek colonies in southern Italy, and then warfare, gradually influenced Roman literary thought and ideals. Greek became the literary language of Rome until the middle of the first century BC when Latin took over. Educated Romans were bilingual in Greek and Latin and were taught in Greek, a not dissimilar position from that in the seventeenth century in England when schools and universities taught in Latin.

Latin also had a smaller vocabulary than Greek making it a less sophisticated mode of communication. Ennius, 239-169 BC, regarded as the father of Roman literature, was primarily an adapter of Greek models and it has been said that "*A play of Ennius was generally a play of Euripides simplified and amplified*". However, for the first time there were Roman books written in Latin.

There was a further and major impediment to Roman literature developing: Alexandria was the centre of the book trade. Alexandria was Greek speaking and the scribes were Greek. It was also the sole centre of papyrus making as the reeds only grow in the Nile delta. That meant booksellers in Rome would have to send manuscripts for copying to Alexandria and pay for the finished items to be freighted back. All these costs made it harder to make a profit, and so local authors were at a distinct disadvantage against the established Greek classics.

Roman literature in Latin had its golden age from about 80 BC to AD 170, which means from Catullus and Sallust to Aulus Gellius and Fronto. The various genres followed the Greek with the one original new form being Roman satire. Unfortunately, no original book scrolls from that period survive in complete form but there are fragments as there are from earlier Greek papyri. The Roman *volumen* was also made of papyrus at this stage, but gradually parchment made into the early form of the book known as a codex became an alternative.

There was a major difference between the Greek and Roman authors. The Greeks believed, whether they were poets, philosophers, or historians, that being an author was an honourable profession. Romans tended to have a day job as a statesman, lawyer or citizen of leisure and their literary work was produced as a pastime. Emperors themselves were often authors and gave prestige to being a writer: Julius Caesar wrote at least two histories; Augustus, Titus and Domitian were poets; Nero performed on stage; and both Hadrian and Julian 'the Apostate' also wrote books. As writers were part of the elite already, writing for money was never an objective. Poets relied on patrons for their income and both Virgil and Horace benefited from such a relationship with Maecenas. One amusing reverse of this is the Roman general Sulla (138-78 BC) who, having received an excruciatingly poor panegyric from a poet, gave the man an honorarium on the condition that he never wrote again.

The Romans, however excellent they may have been in other departments of human activity, had never cared to make the effort necessary to comprehend fully the science of the Greeks, much less add to it. The Roman strength was in practical skills such as engineering and administration and learning was essentially utilitarian. There was a distaste for abstract thought. That the Greeks had excelled in abstract, technical and even impractical subjects meant that they could use Greek accomplishments without having to waste their time doing it all again. Even the architectural writer Vitruvius does not concern himself with weights and stresses or strength of materials, and all his arches were semicircular.

As far as science went, Romans were attracted to encyclopaedic summaries of facts and ideas. Pliny the Elder's (AD23-79) *Historia Naturalis* is a classic such compilation, mainly using earlier texts on geography, geology, botany, zoology, etc. Greek medicine and astronomy were adopted but not developed. Pliny's view was that medicine was not just un-Roman it was Greek. He claimed that doctors earned too much and noted tombstones with inscriptions such as *"A gang of doctors killed me"*, showing that his work has a certain contemporary relevance.

The Roman book trade

Although books on papyrus were principally made in Alexandria, Strabo mentions bookmaking in Rome from 80 BC. The scribes were mainly Greek slaves, although they were well paid and often became close friends of their owners and given considerable responsibility. Writers who copied books were designated *librarii*; correspondence clerks were *amanuenses*; official clerks were *scribae*; those deciphering and transcribing old manuscripts were *antiquarii*; and those taking dictation or reporting speeches or testimony of witnesses were *notarii*.

The best known publisher and bookseller was Pomponius Atticus (110-32 BC) who had a reputation for selling scholarly works. Atticus was wealthy from inheritance and from being a banker. He was also a recognised scholar; his name Atticus derives from his time studying in Athens and love of Greek learning. He had trained a very good team of Roman scribes to make reliable copies of papyrus rolls for writer friends like Cicero and Varro. Other well known publishers were the Sosii brothers who published Horace and Ovid; Tryphon who published Martial and Quintilian; and Secundus, Dorus and Atrectus were also well established in book production.

Very little is known with any certainty about how the book trade worked in Rome. The process of having a book published carried on the Greek practice whereby an author arranged a reading of his work, either with a group of friends or in public, and this *recitatio* of the draft amounted to publication. After that, the draft would accommodate any suggested improvements from comments at the reading and then copies would be written down and distributed. Someone like Cicero would entrust Atticus to make good copies but there was no system of copyright. Unauthorised copying, or piracy, was common, as was plagiarism; and these activities made it still harder for authors to be properly recompensed. Plagiarism is a term first used by Martial and it comes from Roman law where *plagiarus* is a robber or kidnapper. Juvenal takes as the subject of his seventh satire the poverty of men of letters.

Even worse from the author's point of view was that once the new book was in the public domain, inaccurate copies, perhaps made by scribes making notes at the *recitatio,* would circulate. The inaccuracy could be from language problems as slaves were often Greek. Another common custom used by booksellers was for one person to read out loud the text whilst a number of scribes made copies. This could also lead to variations unless thoroughly checked. Counting the number of lines in the original and then the copy was one simple test of accuracy. It is certainly a problem that when manuscripts of ancient writings have been discovered in later times, the version may be far from what the author had intended. And it accounts for why scholars, even in Roman times, would try to hunt down the earliest copies of a book as these were likely to be more authentic than later ones that had become corrupted.

Simple error and variations in text was a problem that scholars could edit out as was done for Homer at the Library of Alexandria. Worse was attributing work to a well-known author to increase sales to the gullible. At one time 130 plays were attributed to Plautus. When Varro got round to editing the list, only 21 were thought to be genuine.

The relationship of bookseller and author in Roman times is unclear; some sources say that an author like Cicero would take a percentage for the copies sold whilst the poet Martial took a fixed sum irrespective of sales. However, there is no clear evidence of this. We do know that Atticus ran a chain of bookshops, *tabernarii*, in Rome and provincial capitals, and that bookshops would have wooden posts outside with attached listings of new works available.

The system of dictating and multiple scribes making copies often led to over production such that even manuscript books on papyrus were remaindered. These copies were sometimes off-loaded to the provinces but also used for wrapping groceries or for lighting fires. Editions were usually not less than 500 and in many cases 1,000. This seems high considering that it took 50 years after printing began in 1455 for editions to reach that size. But then the Roman empire was large and distribution effective. One example of a print run of 1,000 is from the first century AD. Marcus Regulus Aquilius wrote a biography of his young son who had died and he asked for 1,000 copies to be distributed throughout Italy and the provinces.

Bookshops were known in Lyons and Rheims, Carthage in Tunisia and Timgad in Algeria. Horace boasted that his work could be read on the banks of the Bosphorus, in Gaul, Spain and Africa. Propertius claims that his work is known even in the cold countries of the north. Ovid consoled himself in exile that he was read from East to West and was the most widely read author in the world.

By the close of the first century AD, the book trade in the Roman empire was well established. Papyrus was brought from Alexandria; *glutinatores* stuck the papyrus sheets together to make a roll; books were dictated and skilled slaves made copies; others proof-read. In the book shops, the *dilettanti* or collectors bought the books as also did school teachers and the public libraries. Whilst Athens lost its pre-eminence as a centre for higher education by the end of the second century AD, Greek continued as the scholarly language throughout the Roman empire. Attempts were made to set up publishers' rights to protect from piracy.

By the time of the Emperor Constantine, AD 306, Christian literature was taking over from the traditional pagan writing so that scribes and booksellers were no longer producing classical Latin and Greek texts. The transfer of the capital from Rome to Byzantium, completed in AD 328, saw the end of book production in Rome. And the transfer to Byzantium brought Greek back as the official language of the court. Although the western part of the empire staggered on, it was not a peaceful time in Rome which was sacked for the first time in AD 390, again in 410, and then in 476 when Odoacer finally ended the western Roman empire in his conquest of Rome.

Roman literacy

It is thought that between 5% and 30% of the population in Rome was fully literate. Literacy was much higher in the army and the aristocracy, as also amongst the Greek slaves who were often employed as scribes and readers. The education system could have increased this rate, but many writers feel that the elite preferred to keep the rate lower as this enhanced their status and power.

Whereas Greece had a predominantly oral culture, in Rome the spoken word was still dominant but gradually gave way to the written word.

Here in England at the old Roman fort of Vindolanda next to Hadrian's Wall, thin wooden tablets with ink writing were first found in the 1970s. Some 750 have been excavated and they date to about AD100. Much of the content is official army business, but there is correspondence between an officer's wife, Sulpiciana Lepidina, and the wife of an officer commanding a nearby fort which includes a birthday party invitation.

Were libraries well established in Rome?

Private libraries belonging to the wealthy were well established in Rome, eg those belonging to Cicero, Varro, Atticus. Pliny the Elder had a collection of 2,000 books which he would have needed for the *Historia Naturalis* with its 20,000 references from 100 principal authors. One of the very few that have been excavated was the library believed to have belonged to Julius Caesar's father-in-law, Lucius Calpurnius Piso. This was buried in Herculaneum by the eruption of Vesuvius in AD79. It contained some 1,800 papyrus manuscripts about Epicurean philosophy.

Private libraries became fashion statements and status symbols. The contents were often copies of books made by their owners' scribes from originals on loan from friends. Another source was books taken as booty from military conquests, eg the taking of the Macedonian Royal Library in 167 BC, and Sulla taking the library of the Apellicon in 86 BC which contained the remains of the libraries of Aristotle and Theophrastus. Roman libraries were usually divided in two with one part having Greek books and the other Latin.

Book collecting became something of a mania and collectors were often lampooned as people who had no idea of the contents of their library but only arranged the books to impress visitors. Lucian compared them with a donkey which does not prick up its ears at the sound of music. Romans began to seek out and collect early Greek books in the same way that the humanists sought the early manuscripts of classical Greece and Rome in the Italian Renaissance.

The idea of a public library for Rome came from Julius Caesar (100-44 BC) who had admired the library at Alexandria. These were not public libraries as we know them open to all and a refuge for the poor seeking warmth, they were more like a club or society library with entry restricted to the elite and controlled by a doorman. Caesar's vision was implemented by a military friend and follower in 39 BC using books taken from a campaign in Dalmatia. The main growth in public libraries came during the reign of Augustus, 27 BC to AD14, and included the Portico of Octavia in the Campus Martius and the Temple of Apollo on the Palatine Hill. Books in these imperial libraries were still mainly in Greek.

After Augustus, subsequent emperors like Tiberius, Vespasian, and Trajan added more in Rome while Hadrian built his in Athens. By the time of Constantine (AD306-337) there were 28 such public or imperial libraries. All of these libraries were run by state officials and had a budget. We do not know if these were lending libraries; for people to visit in order to make their own copies of a book; or just reading rooms. However, like theatres and baths, they were places to be seen and to socialise. Their appearance would be prestigious with statues or busts of famous authors or gods. Libraries in the provinces were known in Toulouse, Bordeaux, Marseilles, Lyons, Narbonne and Vienne.

These libraries left little by way of a bibliographic legacy as compared with the scholarship of the directors of the Alexandrine library and the bibliographical work of Callimachus. No great scholars were linked to them. Scholarship was handed down through the individual scholars and their tutors.

Libraries in western Europe from the fifth to the eleventh century AD were remarkably consistent in their content. From the Roman villa libraries in Gaul described by Sidonius Apollinaris in the fifth century, to the books known to have belonged to Boethius in the sixth century, to Isidore in the seventh century, to Bede and Alcuin in the eighth century, to Rabanus Maurus and Servatus Lupus in the ninth century, and to Gerbert d'Aurilliac (Pope Sylvester II) in the tenth century, as well as the catalogue of the Bobbio monastery in the same century, all would contain the recognised Christian and patristic works as well as Virgil, Horace, Statius, Plautus, Terence, Varro, both Plinys, Ovid, Juvenal, Seneca, Lucretius, Persius, Martial, Sallust and Suetonius.

By contrast, those libraries left in Rome suffered at the hands of the Goths in AD410 and the Vandals in AD455. Destruction of libraries played a small part in the loss of classical literature, and the next chapter will examine the principal causes.

The Library of Alexandria.

Portrait of a literary woman (possibly Sappho), Pompeii c.50AD,
National Archaeological Museum, Napoli.

II

WHAT WAS LOST AND WHY?

Thank God, it will soon be dark. **Unknown monastic scribe**

It is always hard to estimate what has disappeared if there were no records of what existed in the first place. There were no national deposit libraries or ISBN numbers in ancient times. However, scholars have studied references to Greek and Roman works in contemporary or later writings and casualties have been noted when no copy of the book referred to can be traced. A number of bibliographies, catalogues and anthologies were compiled in ancient and medieval times, such as the *Selections* of Stobaeus (5th century AD), *Bibliotheca* of Photius (AD810–893), and the 31,342 entries in the late tenth century *Suda*. Checking what is extant from these listings gives us some idea of what we have lost.

How many Greek works were lost?

The figure of 75% is one that is frequently used when estimating the amount of Greek literature that has been lost. The earliest fragment of papyrus remaining from ancient Greece is the Derveni papyrus from the beginning of the fourth century BC, a partially burnt allegorical interpretation of an Orphic poem. But as Greek literature began in the ninth century BC, that means there is nothing remaining from the first 500 years even allowing for these years being a largely oral culture. We know that in Athens, 2,000 theatrical works were written and performed between 500 and 200 BC. Today, we can read or perform only 46.

Joannes Stobaeus (fifth century AD) wrote four books of extracts from Greek writers covering poets, historians, orators, philosophers and physicians. The subjects covered range from politics, economics, history, poetry, ethics, medicine, and natural philosophy to simple words of practical wisdom. His work preserves fragments of many authors and works which would otherwise be unknown today: of 1,429 quoted works, only 314 are known to us, which is a loss rate of 78%.

Another more eccentric guide is the *Deipnosophistaí* written in the third century AD by Athenaeus of Naucratis. This is a fictionalised account of table talk in Rome where Greek thought and literature was discussed, and is sometimes known as *The Banquet of the Learned*. The quotations come from 2,500 writings of 700 Greek authors. Frederic George Kenyon, who was head of the British Museum Library from 1909-31, and a noted Classical scholar, calculated that in the section on comic dramatists, only 23 plays are extant despite 366 quotations.

One would expect the works of the less famous writers to become lost over time, but the loss rate of the most well known is extraordinary:

Aeschylus – he is believed to have written some 90 plays, of which six survive. All of these were written later in life so that nothing is left from his most productive 30 years.

Aristophanes – of 40 plays, 11 survive.

Euripides – of 82 plays, 18 survive.

Menander – of over a hundred comedies, only one survives.

Sappho – she wrote around 10,000 lines of poetry; only around 650 survive, mostly in fragments.

Sophocles – of his 123 plays, seven survive.

Aristotle – it is believed that we have about one third of his original works.

Democritus – only citations by later writers are left of the 60 books covering science, mathematics, medicine, music, linguistics, agriculture and art.

Theophrastus – he succeeded Aristotle as Director of the Lyceum and is credited with 227 works, mainly of a scientific nature. Most of his writing is lost except two works on botany and one on petrology.

Strato – followed Theophrastus at the Lyceum and is noted for 40 works on a variety of subjects, but his works on physics built his reputation. None of these survive.

Apollonius – although parts of his work on *Conics* survive, most of his mathematical and astronomical work is lost. He was ranked along with Euclid and Archimedes as one of the three great Hellenistic mathematicians.

Hipparchus – one work survives of all his writing on astronomy, which included work on eclipses, equinoxes and formulating the equivalent of a trigonometrical table.

Philo – four of his nine books in the *Syntaxis mechanicis* survive, covering mechanical inventions.

Virtually nothing except fragments survive from Anaximander,

Cratinus, Heraclitus, Posidonius, or Pyrrhus, the famous general who gave us the term Pyrrhic victory. The writings of the Stoics, Cynics and Skeptics come down to us only as a miscellany of quotations.

Roman losses

To give a scale of what was lost, one estimate is that we have the names of 772 Roman classical authors. Of these, not a word survives from 276 of them. We have fragments ranging from an aphorism to several pages of 352 of the others. Of the remaining 144, we possess at least one of their works but rarely all of them. Only the works of Horace, Virgil, Prosper and Lucretius survive in their entirety with Ovid and Catullus surviving in extensive fragments.

Pliny the Elder wrote seven books but only the *Natural History* survives.

Porphyry (cAD234-305) – only 13 books out of 77 survive. That said, he did not help his chances of a lasting legacy by writing many of his books in favour of paganism and criticising Christianity, his main work being *Against the Christians*. In fact, Theodosius II ordered every copy of this book burned in 435 and again in 448. Everything known about Porphyry's arguments is found in the refutations by Christian apologists, such as Eusebius, Augustine, and Jerome.

Plautus – of about 130 plays (some of questionable authenticity), 20 survive intact

Gaius Petronius – large parts of the *Satyricon* are missing

Livy – 107 of the 142 books of *Ab Urbe Condita, a history of Rome,* are lost.

Varro – estimated to have written 74 works in 620 books; only one work survives complete, although we possess many fragments of the others, mostly in the *Attic Nights* of Gellius. He wrote the one known book on libraries in the ancient world, unfortunately this is one of the lost works.

Surviving remnants are very uneven in their success rates. Copies of Virgil, Cicero, Lucian, Juvenal, Persius, Horace and Ovid are found in relatively large numbers bearing in mind that overall numbers surviving are not at all large. Plautus, Tacitus, Lucretius and Livy are comparatively rare. Many Roman writers have survived only by a single manuscript. The poet Catullus (84-54BC) was famous in his day and was one of a group which Cicero called the "New Poets". Together they made possible the achievement of Horace, Virgil, and Ovid. Of this group, nothing has survived except the 113 poems of Catullus found in a single manuscript in the cathedral library of Verona in 1305.

What caused so many works to be lost?

There were a number of reasons:

a) Poor durability of writing material

It is sobering to reflect that no documents in their original state survive from before AD500 except for a few fragments of papyri buried in Herculaneum by volcanic ash after the eruption of Vesuvius in AD79, the few fragments of papyri found on a rubbish tip in Egypt, and isolated finds like the Derveni fragment. Earlier writing materials like clay with cuneiform writing indented with a stylus survived better, especially if the library they were in was burnt so that the clay baked. This is true of the great library of Assurbanipal at Nineveh which was built around 650BC. But the clay bricks were essentially archives recording transactions rather than contributions to human knowledge. The main exception is the epic Sumerian poem of *Gilgamesh,* written in about 1,800BC, which was found there.

Papyrus was the principal writing material used throughout Classical Greece and Rome. It had been in use in Egypt from about 3,000BC and continued in use until about AD800 when paper took over. Papyrus is made from reeds, and the Nile delta of Egypt was the main source with almost a monopoly. Pliny the Elder in Book 13 of his *Historia Naturalis* gives a very full description of how papyrus grows and is made into a writing material. Reeds were cut and then beaten flat or put in a press. One layer was placed at right angles to the one below and they would stick together as the plant secretes a natural adhesive. The surface was smooth and flexible and could be written on with a reed pen using ink made of lampblack, or crushed minerals diluted in water for coloured ink. It was normal to write on only one side with the scribe choosing the side where the fibres ran horizontally. Papyrus was made in to scrolls by pasting about twenty sheets together with a flour paste used on the small overlap, generally making a scroll of three metres in length, but up to ten metres long. A play by Sophocles or Euripides would fit on a standard three metre roll, as would two books from the *Iliad*. The complete *Odyssey* or *Iliad* would take about thirty six such rolls.

The scroll would be rolled up and read with two hands doing the rolling and unrolling, usually the right hand unrolled and the left folded it back in to a cylindrical shape. It could be stored flat on a shelf or a number kept upright in a leather bucket with a tag attached to the end to identify it. However accomplished the user, a scroll was difficult to handle; hard to search for facts or references; and the continuous script meant no breaks between words and no punctuation. No reader aids such as chapter headings or page numbers were found either.

In Roman times, papyri became more ornate in private libraries. The tags could be projecting knobs of ivory or ebony. The papyrus was smoothed with pumice and treated with cedar oil to inhibit insect damage ; the scroll could be wrapped in purple leather covers with scarlet string and labels. However good the appearance, the rolling and unrolling made them fragile and prone to tearing, as those of us who have folded and unfolded Ordnance Survey maps will be aware. Papyrus kept in Egypt dries out over time and then crumbles . In European conditions the humidity would often lead to mould and so shorten the survival rate to only decades. Papyrus was also prone to insect or rodent damage and could be eaten away. A recently discovered letter from the Greek physician Galen complains that the conditions in Rome were unsuitable for papyrus storage as *"the papyri are completely useless and cannot even be unrolled because they have become glued together by decomposition since the region is both marshy and low-lying, and stifling in summer"*.

This meant that any document would need to be copied at least every two hundred years if it was to survive, and many of the early libraries of Greece and Rome would be staffed with scribes whose job it was to recopy the library's contents. Repeated copying led many scripts to become corrupted over time. Despite all these disadvantages, papyrus was in use by the Arabs until the ninth century AD when paper took over.

Parchment made from animal skin is a much more durable material but was not common before AD 500. It is first mentioned in AD85 and is associated with the transition from the scroll to the codex, the early form of the modern book. The slow transition from the scroll to the codex is shown by fragments of codex forming only 1.5% of archaeological finds in the first and second centuries AD but climbing to 90% by AD500.

A **codex** could be made from parchment or papyrus, Egypt preferring the latter. Scrolls continued to be used for legal documents. The codex had obvious advantages:

- it was more portable and had a greater capacity for text, eg the four Gospels and Acts could be contained in a single codex whereas they would have occupied five separate papyrus rolls;

- it was easier to find and mark a passage by turning pages rather than unrolling a scroll;

- users only needed one hand to read it;

- it was normally bound in wood and was stronger;

- it could be stored more easily on a shelf and labelled on the spine or fore-edge rather than having a label tied to it that could easily become detached.

These advantages were more apparent in non-fiction and reference works such as law, than in works of literature that could often be read through in one go. But, as we will see with the printed book, people are very conservative about change and the scroll persisted for centuries despite the benefits of the codex form.

Very few codices of the first two centuries survive, and these mainly in Egypt. By the third century AD some 100 can be found and 16% are of parchment. That figure rose to 35% in the fourth and fifth centuries. Outside Egypt, no codices survive before the fourth or fifth century AD.

Christians encouraged the codex and it is interesting that hardly any copies of the Bible or other early Christian literature seem to have been made on scrolls. This could be because the codex was first adopted in Rome which hosted an important Christian community. When Constantine effectively adopted Christianity in his reign of AD 306-337, it meant that codices were to be found throughout the Roman empire in churches and schools. Some scholars believe that the Christians used parchment because it was regarded as inferior and they formed a poor community. Others feel that the parchment codex differentiated them from the scrolls uses by the Jews and pagans. It could simply be that experience showed that reference to a passage in the Bible was easier using codex pages than unrolling papyrus scrolls which needed two hands. And codices were more portable, which suited itinerant missionaries.

Papyrus use declines in Europe from the fourth century AD, and ceases when the supply of papyrus was essentially cut off after the Arabs conquered Egypt in AD 642. This made parchment the only choice of material as paper was not known in the West for another 500 years.

b) Lack of copying

The enormous labour of recopying papyrus or parchment inevitably led to questions about what was worth recopying and what could be discarded. It was probably in the fourth century AD that most Roman works were lost. By then the imperial library had decided to copy its papyrus collections on to parchment; an enormous and costly undertaking, both in terms of the much more expensive parchment, but also because it was not possible to write as quickly on parchment as it had been on papyrus. Similar decisions were made about Greek works in the Byzantine empire when parchment replaced papyrus at a slightly later date. Inevitably, to save money some drastic pruning would have occurred with many books not being deemed worth the effort in much the same way that modern libraries discard books to make space.

A lesser fate than total loss was that of summarising and shortening many books to reduce the copying burden. Erasmus felt it highly likely that the loss of all but 36 out of the 142 books of Livy's history of Rome was that the mid second century *Epitome* of Lucius Annaeus Florus, which is much shorter and contains excerpts from Livy, was far quicker to copy. We know that the Emperor Justinian, who ruled from AD 527-565, commanded that the Roman law in some 1,500 documents be reduced and codified in to 50 books forming the *Digest*. What was not included was destroyed. Compilations and miscellanies became popular amongst the elite to reduce their volume of reading and so completeness was never a goal in the way that deposit libraries are today. The compendiums that survive from ancient times such as those of Pliny the Elder, Cassiodorus, Boethius, and Isidore of Seville will be met with in later chapters.

Other reasons for not recopying included:

Prejudice against pagan texts

The early Christian church had an appreciation of the Classical writers and their achievements but nevertheless felt that texts with polytheism might lead to heresy. Christians admired the superiority and sophistication of the ideas, arguments and language of Classical writing and recognised that their own early texts were inelegant. Despite this, Christians were encouraged to restrict their reading to the Bible and Church Fathers. As demand for the Classics lessened, so did the need to recopy them when there was ample demand for the new Christian texts. However, early Christians recognised that they could utilise much of the wisdom from the pagan texts provided that caution and guidance were applied. And so, apart from isolated incidents of the destruction of pagan texts, the Classics were tolerated but lessened in importance over time.

The relationship between Christianity and the Classics was complex. Lactantius (AD250-325) and Tertullian (cAD155-240) both rejected Classical learning. Church Fathers such as Augustine (AD354-430) and Jerome (AD347-420) were steeped in the Classics but felt somewhat guilty about this association. Jerome concluded after his 18 years of translating the Bible in to Latin to produce the Vulgate version which was in use for centuries, that his classical training had been valuable in its production. Augustine rationalised his love of the Classics by the model of the Hebrews taking what they found useful from the Egyptians and so Christians could justifiably appropriate from the Classics, especially Plato, what would enrich their faith.

Origen, Saint Basil and St Gregory of Nazianzus encouraged the young to benefit from the Classics. Origen (AD185-254) had studied under Clement of Alexandria and they both felt that Greek philosophy derived from Hebrew thinking and so a Classical education was essential for understanding Judaism and Christianity. They could see a congruence with Plato who had affirmed divine transcendence, freedom of will, the immortality of the soul, and that virtue is necessary and sufficient for happiness. The ambivalence of Christians towards the Classics is further demonstrated by St Isidore of Seville writing in the early seventh century. He obviously drew on his large library of Classical writers such as the Roman jurists Paulus and Gaius and the Greek medical books of Galen and

Hippocrates when writing his *Etymologies*. But he would not let his monks read them.

There was never any censorship of Classical authors by the Christian church. Besides, as the language of the Roman church was also Latin, the literate and learned could be expected to widen their reading.

More selective academic curricula and different emphases

As the Roman Empire declined during the third century AD, so did intellectual curiosity. The schools had set texts and so we find that copies of these have survived where others have not, eg seven plays by Sophocles and seven by Aeschylus but none of their other works. At a broader level, Romans were very practical and superb engineers. But they lacked the theoretical scientific abilities of their Greek predecessors and so many of the mathematical works were not copied.

Language

When the Roman Empire moved its capital from Rome to Constantinople in AD330, the previous ability of its educated citizens to read both Greek and Latin was largely lost. This divide was made permanent by the Emperor Theodosius' decision to have each of his sons inherit one half of the Empire on his death in AD395. After this event, and the rapid decline of the Western Empire over the course of the fifth century, contact between the two regions became less and less frequent. One consequence of this was a decline in knowledge of Greek in the West, and of Latin in the East. And so within a short while, the number of scribes who could copy in Greek in the West declined as did the demand for Greek texts. Similarly, although the Roman army and administrators could speak Latin in the East, over time their Greek replacements lost the need for Latin and so the Roman classics were not copied there.

It was noted in the last chapter that in the late days of the Library of Alexandria, knowledge of ancient Greek had lessened over 500 years and fewer scribes would be competent to copy it. And the next chapter will see that early Irish manuscripts written in the Insular Latin were not comprehended in monasteries by the later monks.

Books become out of date and were superseded

The need for copying Eratosthenes *Geography* was questioned when the later work of Strabo was seen as more accurate. In more contemporary times, and before national deposit libraries became established, the more ephemeral and lower quality books also disappeared: half of the English novels published between 1770 and 1800, which were the staple of the circulating library, have disappeared. Tapes of many well known television series have been wiped even in our own lifetime: 97 episodes of *Dr Who*.

What are palimpsests?

Many books written on parchment were written over once the original had been wiped clean by washing with milk and oat bran, or more destructively, by wiping with pumice. Parchment was valuable and so it made sense to re-use it when the original was not deemed to be worth keeping. Certain texts would become less used if they went out of date, eg legal texts, or if the language they were written in was no longer understood, which happened with some books in the very early Irish or Insular Latin. In the case of Classical texts, these were at times deemed pagan and so not worth keeping if demand for new Christian texts was high.

One example is Cicero's *De Republica,* the original written over with the psalms of St. Augustine in the seventh century AD at the Bobbio monastery.

II. What was lost and why?

The deliberate destruction of books and libraries

Having your library destroyed has been an occupational hazard for librarians over many centuries. Much of the destruction was in time of war and was either collateral damage, as with the burning of some of the books in Alexandria when Caesar organised an incendiary attack on Greek ships in the harbour, or more of a cultural genocide, as when the Conquistadores destroyed the Aztec painted books in Mexico. The list is endless from Vikings destroying the manuscripts in British and Irish monasteries, to the destruction of 2 million books in the Bosnian National Library in 1992.

Just one case study shows the variety of fates that can befall a famous library. The library at St Benedict's monastery at Monte Cassino was founded in 529. It was destroyed by the Lombards in 570 and the monastery left empty for 150 years. It was burned next by the Arab invaders in 883 and left empty for 50 years. An earthquake destroyed it in 1349. Napoleon's army took their turn to sack it in 1799. However, the contents were saved in the Second World War by the far sighted Wehrmacht officer Lieutenant-Colonel Julius Schlegel. He transferred 70,000 books, 1,200 manuscripts (many of them by Roman classical authors), together with relics and paintings in 120 truckloads for safekeeping in the Vatican. Shortly afterwards, the monastery was destroyed by 570 tons of allied bombing. Fortunately, Schlegel had also saved the blueprints which allowed the rebuilding of Monte Cassino in 1955.

The best overall work on the destruction of books through human history is the one by Baez (2008), who was the Director of the Biblioteca Nacional de Venezuela (see Further Reading list).

Charlemagne (AD 748-814), King of the Franks, 1594. Nicolaes de Bruyn.

III

HOW THE ROMAN CLASSICS SURVIVED

...the ages which deserve an exact enquiry are those times (for such there were) when Ireland was the school of the west, the quiet habitation of sanctity and literature. **Samuel Johnson, 1777**

What happened to the Roman Empire?

The split in the Roman empire began when Constantine moved the capital to Byzantium in AD330. It was consolidated on the death of Theodosius, in AD395, when he divided control over the eastern and western halves between his two sons. Power had by then shifted to the eastern half.

Western Europe was weakened as the Roman army, which had really been the glue that held everything together, was not supported by either the landowning, senatorial aristocrats who preferred the tranquillity of their villas, or by the Roman Catholic church.

The last great emperor in the west was Valentinian I, who ruled from 364-375 using the unpopular army to enforce his rule. On his death, the administration was taken over by the cronyism and amateurism of the landowning elite and the bishops who tended to view Rome with disdain for its pagan past. The previously thriving school system, that ensured thousands of educated young men had a knowledge of the Roman classics, disappeared; and a knowledge of the Classics became restricted to private libraries of the elite and the upper echelons of the Catholic Church.

This weakness was noted by the barbarians who had looked in at the more developed Roman empire in the west and wanted to feel part of it. Their invasions were more those of economic migrants and were far less destructive than the true warrior invasions that came later. Visigoths crossed the frontier at the Danube in 376; Vandals entered Spain and Gaul in 406-9; Burgundians took over the Rhone in 430. The eastern Roman empire defending the Balkans was smarter at dealing with the barbarians. They resorted to absorbing some in to the army, and using cash to buy the others off if force did not work.

In the west, having seen the northern frontier collapse, the Emperor Honorius moved the capital from Rome to the well defended Ravenna in 402. This was prescient as the Visigoths under Alaric invaded and sacked Rome in 410. As sackings go, this was a somewhat gentle three day affair with most of the main buildings left intact. And by this time, many of the populace could see little difference between the Roman army and the invader and so they just treated the barbarian with the same contempt as they had the Roman soldier. The difference was that the taxes from land and agriculture that had kept the government going were now lost. Without functioning civil administration in the period after these conquests, there was no funding for libraries and centres of learning so that the system of education requiring a knowledge of Latin classics collapsed. Schools, libraries and academies closed.

The Roman Empire in the west effectively came to an end in 476 when the last Emperor, Romulus Augustulus, was defeated by the Ostrogoths. The Ostrogoths were the eastern branch of the Germanic Goths and their heartland stretched from the Black Sea to the Baltic. Their leader in Italy was Theodoric who ruled from 493-526 with Ravenna as his capital. His reign began the transition from the Ancient to the Medieval world.

The population of Rome itself shrank from over a million to as low as 30,000. Officials in the Roman army, government and business adopted the styles and customs of the conquering Ostrogoths which placed less value on education. Scholarship was taken over by the Church as it at least had a functioning apparatus. This meant that much of the new literature being written was no longer secular. It comprised studies, commentaries and interpretations of the Bible, as well as discussion on the nature of religion, heresy, etc. The great Christian authors writing in Greek were Basil and Eusebius, whereas Augustine and Jerome wrote in Latin. The existing libraries in the Empire found it hard to absorb such new material and the Christian writing collected in churches and then in the new monasteries. Many of the books in Rome had been moved to Constantinople in AD330 when the capital moved. Those books from the old private libraries that still survived, mainly in Rome, Verona and Ravenna, were being taken to monasteries and then copied in their scriptoria. But the Church was at this time largely hostile to pagan literature so that the combination of destruction and hostility gave the Latin classics a bleak future.

A good number of Roman titles did not survive until 500, especially early works by writers such as Ennius, Lucilius and Naevius and orators before Cicero. This may well be because of a decline in popularity which meant that they ceased being copied.

Why did Monasteries become important?

Monasteries were first developed in the desert of southern Egypt near Thebes in the early fourth century AD by Pachomius (282–348), Paul of Thebes (died c345), and Anthony of Egypt (d.356). Pachomius drew up a code of behaviour for monks demanding poverty, asceticism and unconditional obedience to the abbot. The idea spread quite rapidly so that new monasteries formed throughout Egypt and then throughout the Eastern Roman Empire. St Basil, the bishop of Caesarea, was the prime mover in this spread and he advocated monks studying both Christian and Classical literature.

Monks had to be literate or be willing to become literate, and so the monasteries needed books. But the monastery libraries in the Eastern Empire tended to be small, perhaps 100 books, and these contained about 95% Christian texts with only a few books of Classical writers. As such, they played little part in the survival of the Classics unlike the palace, academic and private libraries of the East that aided preservation of Greek learning.

One of the most influential of the early monasteries was named Vivarium near Squillace in Calabria, southern Italy. It was founded by **Cassiodorus** (c490–c585) on his family land in about 550 just after he had retired. Cassiodorus has been called the last Roman and the first Medieval man. He was Roman by training, such that both he and his father had been members of the Roman senate, but had spent almost twenty years in Constantinople studying religion. He had transferred allegiance to become a senior civil servant in the administration of Theodoric, the new Ostrogothic ruler in Ravenna, even becoming his chief adviser. He was one of the last of the scholarly bureaucrats of the late Roman empire and initiated the aristocratic ideal of cultivated leisure into his new monastery.

Cassiodorus had hoped to work with Pope Agapetus to create a Christian university in Rome on the model of the Museum and library in Alexandria, but the fourth Sack of Rome in 546 ruined his ambition. Cassiodorus was a scholar and a visionary who saw that the monasteries acted as educational oases in the turmoil around them and had a role in preserving intellectual continuity. In his view, power would pass from the warring kings and army generals to the Church. He hoped that his new monastery could help to act as a bridge between eastern and western Christianity, Roman and Gothic rule, through teaching and a collection of books in both Latin and Greek which he had accumulated in his long political career. The size of the library has been estimated at 300 books.

Cassiodorus founded a scriptorium for the copying of these books at Vivarium. In this he was ahead of the Benedictines who followed his example. Vivarium was not Benedictine but followed a somewhat looser rule set down by St. John Cassian (c360–c435), one of the original desert monks and ascetics who brought monasticism to parts of southern France and is buried at the Monastery of St. Victor near Marseilles. Cassiodorus wrote a book, *Institutiones*, which set out what he regarded as the suitable content for a monastic library and it included cosmography, geography, medicine, rhetoric and Classical literature along with scripture, patristic writing and church history. It acted as a bibliographical survey of the literature of the time. This book guided many other monasteries throughout the Medieval period and in doing so, transmitted the interests of antiquity to the medieval monastery.

It was the view of Cassiodorus that the monk who copied Christian texts *"with his hand preaches to men, with his fingers loosens their tongues, without speaking gives salvation to mortals, with pen and ink fights against the unlawful temptations of the devil."* It was Cassiodorus who achieved acceptance of the idea that scribal work was labour and so a legitimate occupation for a monk. He could see that whereas Romans had managed to have slaves copy books for them, in a monastery there was time for monks to become scribes reproducing manuscripts which would far surpass in quality those of the copyists of Rome.

Cassiodorus set an example to his monks by copying a Psalter and some of the books of the Bible. And he continued his early historical writings by making Biblical commentaries. His last book, *De Orthographia*, which showed monks how to correct ancient manuscripts and emphasised the importance of punctuation, was written when he was ninety three. By transferring his services to the Church, he sensed that the Church would provide a good future for an organised society and continued civilisation, thus leading to the preservation and cultivation of Classical literature. The fate of the books in the Vivarium library is not known, but has provided speculation and theories for many scholars through the ages. This area of southern Italy became increasingly Greek with refugees from Antioch and Alexandria, a point that will be made again in the next chapter.

Another civil servant under Theodoric was **Boethius** (480–525) who had received a Classical education in Athens. He had also benefited from marrying a descendant of Symmachus the Orator (345–402), who was the last pagan statesman in Rome holding out against Christianity. Symmachus had left a large library in his palace and in which Boethius studied. Recognising that the Greco-Roman civilisation was dying, he had intended to translate into Latin the works of Plato and Aristotle. Unfulfilled in this ambition, he did translate from the Greek treatises on arithmetic, geometry, mechanics, astronomy, philosophy and music from Aristotle, Porphyry and Euclid. It was this work, endlessly copied until the twelfth century, that enabled scholars in western Europe to have some awareness of what had been lost from ancient Greek thought.

A Christian condemned to death by Theodoric for allegedly plotting against the throne, Boethius wrote his famous work *The Consolation of Philosophy* whilst in the condemned cell. He relied on his Classical training in writing this but he is seen as a bridge between a dying Classical civilisation and a nascent Christian one.

Slightly earlier than the founding of the monastery at Vivarium, **St Benedict of Nursia** founded the famous monastery at Monte Cassino in 529. St Benedict was influential by defining his Rule, in 73 short chapters, which provided a complete code of monastic duty. It encouraged and governed many more monastic institutions in the succeeding years. Chapter 48 enjoined monks to read for two hours a day and made provision that at the beginning of Lent, each monk would be given a book to read right through during the coming year. Because of this requirement, books multiplied in the scriptoria and many Benedictine institutions developed large libraries. In later years, the Benedictine monasteries were the principal places of education before the universities were founded in the twelfth century, and these monasteries were key to the survival of Latin classics even though the church regarded them as pagan works.

How did the Irish become involved in this monastic influence?

In the West, monasteries were known as early as 361 in Gaul when Martin of Tours established Ligugé Abbey. He later founded Marmoutier Abbey outside Tours in 372. St Patrick of Ireland visited Marmoutier but studied principally at the Auxerre monastery, founded in 422, and received his tonsure at Lérins monastery which was founded in 410. Although monasteries were first founded in Europe in Gaul, it was the experience of Irish missionary monks who studied in them that saw their later growth in many of the countries in western Europe including the islands of Britain and Ireland. Between 575 and 725 the Irish founded about 150 monasteries outside Ireland and they became centres of scholarship as Cassiodorus had foreseen.

Ireland, the farthest western reach of Europe, had never been part of the Roman Empire. Christianity had been brought to Ireland even before its supposed conversion by St Patrick in 432. This is obvious because Palladius was sent by Pope Celestine I in 431 to be the bishop for the Christians already influenced by early missionaries from Britain. However, Ireland was a very rural and tribal country with no major centres of population that could be deemed towns let alone cities. And the episcopal model required a sizeable urban population. For whatever reason, Palladius had little success.

The real evangelising was done by St Patrick, the son of a wealthy middle class Romano-British father. Patrick is believed to have been captured in 403 by Irish raiders and spent six years in slavery as a shepherd in Co. Antrim before escaping back to England. His faith had deepened in his enforced exile and he went on to study in French monasteries and eventually to be ordained. He returned as a missionary to Ireland where he is recognised as the country's patron saint. St Patrick was a preacher and organiser rather than a man of letters.

Irish Christianity was not consciously in opposition to that of Rome, but it was independent of the Roman hierarchy and strictures. It was always monastic rather than episcopal, because there were no major urban centres and had an independence from Rome. Numerous monasteries were founded in the sixth century such as Armagh (457), Clonard (520), Glendalough (c.540), Clonmacnoise(544-8), Kells (550), Durrow (553), Clonfert (557), and Bangor (559). Irish monks preserved an uncorrupted Latin and encouraged scholarship, particularly in grammar and interpretative religious texts.

Many texts survived in Ireland as they were brought by scholars fleeing westward from Europe, especially Gaul, to avoid the barbarian invasions in the early fifth century. This was especially true of the monks from Auxerre, Lérins, and Marmoutier because of their already close links with their Irish brethren. Lérins was known to have copies of Cicero, Virgil and Xenophon amongst others. These monks brought with them texts in classical Greek as well as Latin. The Irish had an existing literary tradition and the monks were happy to blend this with Christian texts as well as Roman and a few Greek classics. There was none of the agonising of St Jerome as to the compatibility of pagan and Christian texts;

whatever encouraged learning was welcome and so imposing self-censorship made no sense to them. This breadth and richness of Irish monastic learning equipped them well for their future role in the history of western culture.

Kenneth Clark, in his famous television series *Civilisation* of 1969, begins with an episode titled "*By the skin of our teeth*". The episode starts with film of early monastic settlements off the western coast of Ireland and the quote,

"It is hard to believe that for quite a long time - almost a hundred years (ie mid fifth century to mid sixth century) western Christianity survived by clinging to places like Skellig Michael, a pinnacle of rock eighteen miles from the Irish coast, rising to seven hundred feet out of the sea."

Many of the early Irish monasteries founded in the sixth century effectively became what amounted to universities. They welcomed students from all over Britain as well as the continent attracted by the hospitality, teaching and libraries. St Bede (673-735), the historian and himself a monk, notes that they welcomed commoners and nobles and not just those willing to become monks. There was still a wariness about the Celtic Christianity of Ireland as noted by Aldhelm, who was Abbot of Malmesbury and later the Bishop of Sherborne. He had been educated by Maeldub, the Irish monk who founded what would become Malmesbury Abbey in 661 and then succeeded him in 675. He warned a young Saxon student about to go to Ireland of the ancient fables and temptations of Irish education:

"What advantage does it bring to the sacrament of the orthodox faith to sweat over reading and studying the polluted lewdness of Proserpine, or Hermione, the wanton offspring of Menelaus and Helen, or the Lupercalia and the votaries of Priapus?".

Clonard Abbey, founded by St Finian and now in Co. Meath, was one of the foremost educational establishments. All of these monasteries had libraries and scriptoria where books were copied to be used for teaching or to send to new monasteries. It is said that there were 3,000 students at Clonard. These included the Twelve Apostles of Ireland, some of the most distinguished of the early monks, many of whom went on to found new monasteries. Of these, St Columba (521–97) is well known as the founder of the monastery at Iona on the west coast of Scotland in 563.

Why did Irish monks feel the need to travel abroad?

The Irish monastic tradition was not one of quiet contemplation but of a restless, missionary need to travel and bring their Christianity to new lands. Normally travelling in bands of twelve, they brought Christianity back to parts of Europe ransacked by various barbarian invasions in the next one hundred years founding innumerable monasteries which would be centres of learning. These were normally set in unused land in depopulated areas. As well as learning, they improved agriculture, drained marshland, built roads and promoted arts and crafts. The collapse of the Roman empire had meant the loss of schools, libraries and churches which were neither valued nor funded by the invaders.

One of the most famous of the missionary monks was St Columban (or Columbanus), 540–615, who travelled from Ireland to found monasteries on the continent arriving in Brittany in 585. Columbanus had studied at Bangor Abbey. He founded his first monastery at Annegray in Burgundy. This proved so popular that he had to found two more nearby of which Luxeuil is the better known. His popularity caused jealousy in the existing French clerical hierarchy which had bishops in the Roman tradition. They soon found cause to complain as their tradition of dating Easter was different from the Irish one and the Irish form of tonsure also differed from the Roman one. Columbanus found himself at odds with Burgundian royalty and was banished back to Ireland. But his ship did not make it, and he travelled through Germany and Switzerland to Italy where he founded a monastery at Bobbio (which was reputedly the model used by Umberto Eco for *The Name of the Rose*) in 614.

Columbanus is buried at Bobbio. During his twenty five years of missionary work in France, Germany, Switzerland and Italy it is thought he founded at least sixty monasteries. He also left behind letters, poems and sermons notable for their playful imitation of, or quotations from, Classical writers including Sappho, Virgil, Ovid, Juvenal, Martial. He also reintroduced through their scriptoria and libraries a new awareness of Classical learning.

On his travels through Switzerland, he was forced to part with one of his companions, Gall (c550-640), who was left behind. St Gall had also studied at Bangor. This Irish monk himself became famous and was offered a bishopric in Constance or of going back to Luxeuil as abbot. But he refused and became a central figure in developing the Swiss Church. The monastery of St Gall was built after his death and became distinguished by its library and scriptorium.

Between 575-725, the Irish founded 113 monasteries and schools in France and Switzerland; 26 in Germany; 10 in Austria; and 3 in northern Italy.

A number of Irish monks also founded monasteries in Germany at an even later date. These were not the evangelising monks of the earlier wave from Ireland, but Benedictines , mainly from northern Ireland, seeking escape from the subjugation of their homeland by the English. This new wave founded monasteries in Ratisbon (Regensburg) in 1111; Wurzburg in 1134; Nuremberg in 1140; Constance in 1142; St George at Vienna in 1155; Eichstadt in 1183; and St Mary in Vienna in 1200.

Was Irish scholarship valued?

The breadth of scholarship found in the Irish monasteries, both in Ireland and those founded on the continent, can be seen in the regard in which the later monks were held in the Carolingian Renaissance which will be looked at shortly. The monks from Ireland in the ninth century were often fleeing the Viking invasions that destroyed many of their monasteries over the period 795-1014. One attraction was the famous palace school at Aachen established by Charlemagne (748-814). This was directed by Alcuin from York (735-804), doubtless the most learned man of his time, and he is thought to have been partly educated at Clonmacnoise. Other teachers at the school from Ireland were St Clement (750-818) who was then sent to found a palace school in Paris. Dicuil (c755-c825) was best known as an astronomer and geographer writing books on the former subject in 814 and the latter in 825.

Johannes Scotus Eriguena (815-77) was the most eminent of the scholars at court after Alcuin and later succeeded him as head of the Aachen palace school. Alcuin was a famous teacher, but Eriguena was an original thinker and philosopher. It was Eriguena who was asked by Charlemagne's grandson to translate the Greek copy of Dionysius the Areopagite given by Pope Paul I to King Pippin in about 758. The Irish were known to be amongst the very few scholars in Europe in the Dark Ages who could read Greek.

Dungal, a monk from Bobbio, was asked by Charlemagne to explain two solar eclipses in 810 and it is thought his knowledge of Pliny and Macrobius enabled him to do this. One of Charlemagne's grandchildren asked him to set up a school in Pavia which is where history associates him. Sedulius Scotus (fl. 840-60) taught at the cathedral school in Liège, was known to be fluent in Greek, and wrote a treatise on Aristotle. St Vergilius (c700-784) had been abbot of Aghaboe, Co. Laois, but later went on to be bishop of Salzburg. He was a geographer and astronomer.

(It should be noted that the term "Scotus" rather confusingly denotes of Irish origin. Until about 1000, Ireland was known as Scotia. After the eleventh and twelfth centuries, Scotia refers to what we now call Scotland. The date has especially to be taken into account as famous Franciscan theologians such as Duns Scotus (1266-1308) were, indeed, of Scottish birth).

What part did monastic scriptoria play?

Monasteries in Europe had been associated with the making of manuscript books from 550 when Cassiodorus established Vivarium. Transcribing manuscripts was held under monastic rules to be a full equivalent of manual labour in the fields. Some monks obviously enjoyed the work and would work by candlelight into the night at the expense of their eyesight. One such was Emo of Friesland (c1175-1237) who was recorded spending his nights when Abbot of Wittewierum monastery illuminating the choir books.(He is the first recorded foreign student at Oxford University). Others found it painful and there is evidence that scribal work could be used as a punishment. A quote from the monastery at St Gall says, *"He who does not know how to write imagines it to be no labour, but although these fingers only hold the pen, the whole body grows weary."* Sitting on a backless stool for six hours a day would have been uncomfortable. And many of the northern European monasteries were bitterly cold in winter as few had heating. Scribes were not always happy with their lot and sometimes appended comments to their script. Collected examples include:

- *Writing is excessive drudgery. It crooks your back, it dims your sight, it twists your stomach, and your sides.*

- *St Patrick of Armagh, deliver me from writing.*

- *As the sick man desireth health even so doth the scribe desire the end of the volume.*

- *Now I've written the whole thing: for Christ's sake give me a drink.*

However, not all scribes were unhappy with their lot. In the ninth century, an Irish monk would compile a commonplace book in the scriptorium at St Gall (or possibly at Reichenau) with excerpts from the *Aeneid*, hymns, works of the Church Fathers, some Greek and natural history and the famous poem, written in Old Irish, to his cat, Pangur Bán:

I and Pangur Bán my cat,
'Tis a like task we are at:
Hunting mice is his delight,
Hunting words I sit all night.

Better far than praise of men
'Tis to sit with book and pen;
Pangur bears me no ill-will,
He too plies his simple skill.

'Tis a merry task to see
At our tasks how glad are we,
When at home we sit and find
Entertainment to our mind.

Oftentimes a mouse will stray
In the hero Pangur's way;
Oftentimes my keen thought set
Takes a meaning in its net.

'Gainst the wall he sets his eye
Full and fierce and sharp and sly;
'Gainst the wall of knowledge I
All my little wisdom try.

When a mouse darts from its den,
O how glad is Pangur then!
O what gladness do I prove
When I solve the doubts I love!

So in peace our task we ply,
Pangur Bán, my cat, and I;
In our arts we find our bliss,
I have mine and he has his.

Practice every day has made
Pangur perfect in his trade;
I get wisdom day and night
Turning darkness into light

Irish monk, ninth century. Translated from Old Irish.

Although there is some evidence that in early monasteries it was the feebler monks who were assigned to writing books whilst their fitter colleagues worked in the fields, in later times it was often the more scholarly who worked in the scriptorium. Indeed, in the seventh and eighth centuries in Irish monasteries, the murder of a scribe had the same penalty as killing a bishop or an abbot. A scribe was regarded as doing God's work and received recognition after death. One story is from the monastery at Wedinghausen in Westphalia where an English monk spent twenty years writing holy books. When his tomb was opened twenty years after his death, his body had crumbled to dust except for his writing hand which was found intact and then preserved as a relic beneath the altar.

What materials did a scriptorium require?

The material for making books was normally produced on the premises. Monks were provided with desks, parchment, ink, pens, penknives, pumice stone for smoothing the parchment, awls and rulers for making guide lines, and reading frames for holding the original to be copied. That parchment was expensive is noted many times in monastic archives and some of the lesser establishments simply could not afford it. Many monasteries would provide funds for the scriptorium from the income of certain land or water mills. In France, priests holding benefices would pay a tax to support book production. However, re-using parchment was not uncommon. Palimpsests were noted in the previous chapter and the period 550-750 is when many of them were created.

As parchment was valuable, it made sense to re-use it when the original was not thought to be worth keeping. In the case of Classical texts, these were at times deemed pagan and so not worth keeping if demand for new Christian texts was high. In the monasteries founded by the Irish there were particular reasons why texts became less used. The original Latin that survived from its exclusion from the Roman Empire, Insular Latin, was not understood very well on the continent. Hence books made in Ireland and brought to Europe were often casualties of erasure. This was noted at Luxeuil and Bobbio, both Irish foundations, and Classical texts were common casualties. The original Classical texts remained faintly legible, so that modern fluorescent and spectral imaging techniques and photography have aided further recovery. Some of the works of Plautus and Terence, Cicero and Livy, both Elder and Younger Pliny, Sallust and Seneca, Virgil and Ovid, Lucan, Juvenal, Gellius, Persius and Fronto have been recovered from palimpsests.

An early American palaeographer, E.A. Lowe (1879-1969) was having trouble distinguishing between Irish manuscripts and those of the early monastic foundations in Northumbria. He, somewhat unkindly, offered advice to his students that:

- *if a manuscript looks untidy and messy*
- *if the number of lines varies wildly from page to page*
- *if the ruling is missing or, if present, disregarded*
- *if the parchment is rough to the touch or very greasy*
- *if odd or irregular scraps of parchment are used*

then it is most likely to be Irish.

How quickly could monks write a book?

The speed at which monks could write a book has been the subject of much debate. The length of daylight changed during the year so that productivity was lower in the winter. The demands of prayer and other monastic routines would limit scribal time. In general, it is thought that the Roman practice of one person dictating while others made copies was rare. Alcuin was known to have trained scribes in this way when he became Abbot of Tours in his retirement, but, training aside, each monk or nun would work at his or her own pace. All the monastic orders kept silence in their scriptoria. Writing three to four pages a day seems a working average, with three to four books completed in a year depending on the size of the book.

If a copy had to be made urgently, the practice was to apportion several monks to share the task which is why some books have evidence of different handwriting in the finished product. Books would be passed to a corrector, an early version of a proof-reader, to check that an exact copy had been made. Whilst this would stop further errors, or where a monk thought he could "improve" the text, if the original was poor, it could not stop replicating a corrupted text. However, the Carolingian Renaissance did attempt critical practice and to establish uncorrupted and near original versions of text.

Where were books written?

Benedictines preferred a collective scriptorium with perhaps a dozen monks writing together. This room sometimes combined the library. Cistercians and Carthusians favoured small cells and individual scriptoria. In English monasteries, the cloisters were usually used with niches or carrels allocated for each monk to set up his stool beneath a cloister window and use the built in wood or stone surface; Gloucester Cathedral has a good example in stone. However, in the fourteenth and fifteenth centuries there was a move away from this towards a designated scriptorium.

Copies would be made of books in the monastery's own library. This could be to guarantee enough copies for the annual distribution at Lent; to have duplicate copies to exchange with other monasteries or to give as gifts which might encourage return favours; and there is some evidence that copies were made for sale in later times. Written records show an active inter-library loan service with other monasteries whereby books requested by a senior figure could be borrowed and then copied by monks in the home scriptorium. This was achieved by offering sizeable deposits as guarantees of return or by bartering some of the duplicate library copies that had been made. Servatus Lupus (805-862), who was Abbot of Ferrières, was especially known as an active inter-library borrower. He is regarded as an early humanist and had an especial interest in Roman classical authors. He would borrow other copies of books he already had in order to compare and collate them as well as requesting books he had not read. A number of his manuscripts in distinctive Caroline style of Cicero, Livy, Gellius, Macrobius, Donatus and Valerius Maximus survive.

By the thirteenth century, many monasteries were producing fewer books as there were fewer scribes. Even the monastery of St Gall could not find any scribes in 1297, whereas Fulda was recorded as having 40 scribes in the mid-eighth century. A number of reasons could be suggested. Principally, lay scribes were taking over the work in the commercial cities with universities, and professional scribes were reliable. The near monastic monopoly of book production had gone forever.

The introduction of printing in the 1450s did not see an immediate reduction in scribal work. Johann of Trittenheim (Trithemius) was the Abbot of Sponheim and he was very vocal in rejecting printing and espoused the virtue of manuscript books on parchment until he died. However, a number of monasteries welcomed printing and even set up presses themselves. St Albans in England was one of the earliest with a press on the premises. The earliest printing press in Italy was at Subiaco, a Benedictine foundation, but it was run for only a few years by two itinerant German printers as will be noted in Chapter 7. In the Netherlands, The Brethren of Common Life, a Catholic organisation that ran on monastic lines but without taking vows, actively printed religious books in the vernacular from its invention through to the Reformation. Both Thomas à Kempis and Erasmus were linked to the Brethren.

How important were monastic libraries?

None of the libraries in the early monasteries were large and very few catalogues are extant. Fortunately, there remain catalogues of Reichenau, Bobbio and St Gall from the ninth century. Reichenau had 415 volumes; Bobbio had 666; and St Gall about 700. Individual monks may also have had their own books as is known when they were bequeathed to the library. The library books covered theology in its broadest sense, but also grammar, metrics, astronomy and medicine as well as Classical literature. **Bobbio** had copies of Horace, Virgil, Ovid, Juvenal, Martial, Perseus, Terence, Cicero, Lucan, Valerius Flaccus, Claudian, Seneca, Pliny the Elder, Demosthenes and Aristotle as well as mathematical and historical works. **Corbie** records copying of Cicero, Virgil, Tacitus, Horace, Suetonius, Sallust, Livy, Seneca, Pliny the Elder, Martial and Ovid. A sixteenth century catalogue of **Fulda** lists Sallust, Lucian, Cicero, Livy, Virgil, Plautus, Aristotle and Ovid. Reichenau, St Denis, Lorches and Monte Cassino also had Pliny the Elder.

The library at **St Gall** became a hunting ground for early Italian humanists such as Poggio Bracciolini (1380-1459). During the nearby Council of Constance from 1414-18, there were enforced breaks which enabled these scholars to visit monasteries and search the libraries for early Classics. By fair means or foul, these were then copied and sent back to Italy to be read by other humanists. Poggio writes that he found copies of the works of Cicero, Priscian, Quintilian, Statius, *The Argonautica* of Gaius Valerius Flaccus, and commentaries of Asconius Pedianus, at St Gall. More will be written about Poggio in Chapter 6 which looks at humanism and the Italian Renaissance.

Monasteries in the east have also proved valuable quarries for scholars. As late as 2005, a postdoctoral student discovered in the Vlatadon monastery in Thessalonica a parchment manuscript of Galen. The *De Indolentia*, or *On the Avoidance of Grief*, describes Galen's response to the loss of many of his own writings and collected works in a fire at the Temple of Peace in Rome in 192. This letter/treatise shows how moral philosophy was discussed by doctors at the time and has elicited conferences and a vast literature since its discovery.

When did the Benedictines take over all monasteries?

St Benedict of Nursia founded the monastery at Monte Cassino in 529. He also founded monasteries at Subiaco, near Rome, and some thirteen others in Italy in the sixth century. These monasteries all followed the Benedictine Rule which was much less severe than the Irish one adopted by Columbanus which involved corporal punishment and self-mortification. Eventually the Benedictine Rule was adopted by all of the early monasteries, including the Irish ones outside Ireland, owing to the influence of Pope Gregory I (d. 604) and then the Emperor Charlemagne (742-814). By 725, all monasteries followed the Benedictine Rule which encouraged the making of books.

Other monastic orders such as the Carthusians, Cistercians, and Cluniacs, were all founded some 300 years later. These orders also had scriptoria and libraries but they restricted their output to religious books. The making of books by Classical writers was only done in Benedictine and Augustinian institutions.

As was noted at the end of Chapter 2, Monte Cassino was sacked several times. It came back to prominence under the abbacy of Desiderius (1058-87). He actively sought out books for copying throughout Italy and other parts of the old Roman empire, and these included pagan and scientific works. Copies of some titles by Apuleius and Tacitus only survive from this eleventh century revival at Monte Cassino.

What was the later Anglo-Saxon Mission?

In 668, the Greek speaking Theodore of Tarsus arrived in Britain to be Archbishop of Canterbury. He came with another learned man, Adrian, originally from North Africa, who was to become the Abbot of St Augustine's in Canterbury. They brought with them many books from Rome, including pagan classics, and an agenda to introduce a mainly literary educational programme. The teaching, especially of Virgil, Persius and Juvenal, spread throughout southern England.

This development in turn led to a number of monks from southern parts of England being sent on a mission to Frisia, what is now largely the Netherlands and part of Germany. The most famous is St Boniface (c675-754) who was born in Crediton, Devon. He was made Archbishop of Mainz by the Pope with jurisdiction over all dioceses east of the River Rhine. Boniface was responsible for founding in 744 the very influential monastery at Fulda, in the state of Hesse, and he is buried there. It can be argued that Boniface brought a renewal of learning to Germany some fifty years in advance of the Carolingian Renaissance.

St Walburga (c710-777), a nun, also from Devon, was educated for twenty six years at Wimborne Minster. As the niece of St Boniface, she joined him on the continent to help convert the pagan Germans along with her brothers, St Willibald and St Winibald. One of the churches named after her is in the Netherlands at Zutphen. It is a fascinating coincidence that both Zutphen and Wimborne Minster have two of the very few chained libraries left in Europe.

Other famous monks of this second wave are Willibrord (c658–739), who was Northumbrian in origin. He is known as the Apostle of Frisia and became the first Bishop of Utrecht. He founded the monastery of Echternach, which is now in Luxembourg, in 698. For twelve years he had studied in Ireland at an Anglo-Saxon monastery in Co. Carlow. There was extensive correspondence from the monks in Frisia requesting books from England.

Monasteries in Northern England

At about the same time as the developments from Canterbury in the south, a monastery was founded by Benedict Biscop at Wearmouth in Northumbria in 674/5. Biscop had travelled to Rome in 653 and returned full of enthusiasm for the church. He spent the years 665/7 at the monastery of Lérins off the coast of Provence, where he was impressed by the Benedictine rule and the library. He changed his name to Benedict. He returned to Britain with Theodore of Tarsus and was made Abbot of the Benedictine monastery of SS. Peter and Paul's in Canterbury in 669. Northumbria, however, was Biscop's home and after two years in Canterbury, he began to build a monastery at Wearmouth which combined with a sister monastery at Jarrow a few years later. The combined monastery became famous for its scriptorium. The *Codex Amiatanus,* which weighs thirty four kilos and is the earliest complete Vulgate Bible in existence, was written here.

The most famous pupil of the combined monastery was Bede (c672–735), best known for his history of the early church in England, but also a writer on theology and science. His extensive writings show a familiarity with Ovid, Lucretius, Virgil, Pliny the

Elder and Horace. It was a pupil of Bede, Egbert, who founded the cathedral school at York where Alcuin (c735-804) studied and then became the master. Alcuin notes that at York Minster, the library had works by Aristotle, Sedulius, Juvenal, Virgil, Lucan, Statius, Donatus, Priscian, and Servius, amongst others; the Greek writers probably in Latin translation.

Shortly after the Frisian mission, many of the large libraries at centres such as York, Canterbury and Wearmouth were destroyed in the Viking invasions from 793-1035. No catalogue of an English library exists before the Norman invasion and so we only have references from the writing of Alcuin, Bede and other historians to guide us as to what books were available before the Viking raids.

All of these foundations had encouraged the making of books and formation of libraries. Their surviving books travelled by copying, gift, sale, theft or looting to form the core of new libraries in the Late Middle Ages and the Renaissance.

That Anglo-Saxon and Celtic scholarship was pre-eminent at this time is shown by Charlemagne's choice of Alcuin to move from York Minster to his court at Aachen to be Master of the Palace School. Most of Europe during the sixth and early seventh centuries was hostile to pagan culture, although many Classical texts still survived in private and religious libraries in Italy. It was the three strands from the British Isles: the Irish, the Canterbury led movements in the south and the Tyne/Wear and York axis in the north; that came together to provide the educated men and books to support Charlemagne bring about his educational renaissance in western Europe. In turn, this allowed long lost books from Italy to resurface.

The Carolingian Renaissance

The empire of Charlemagne brought what was hardly a Renaissance, but it did provide a pause in the decline of the West. He became King of the Franks in 768 and then of the Lombards. In 799 Pope Leo made him Holy Roman Emperor. He brought together much of western Europe to form an empire not seen since the Romans had left some 300 years before. A large empire required educated civil servants and clergy and Charlemagne recognised that educational standards had slipped dramatically during the period we know as the Dark Ages. He opened schools, for the first time in centuries, at the monasteries and cathedrals as well as bringing learning to his own court. He became the first monarch in Europe, possibly the world, to introduce universal, free primary education.

As the most learned man in Europe, Alcuin was chosen to head this educational mission. Alcuin arrived at the court in Aachen in 782 and stayed until 790. His task was to develop basic literacy in the schools as well as improve higher studies at the Palace School. In 787, a proclamation was issued by Charlemagne and sent to all the bishops and abbots in his kingdom explaining the need to improve educational standards and what they must do to achieve this. The document would have been written mainly by Alcuin. A second proclamation of 789 declared, *"As it is our desire to improve the condition of the Church, we make it our task to restore with the most watchful zeal the study of letters, a task almost forgotten through the neglect of our ancestors. We therefore enjoin on our subjects, so far as they may be able, to study the liberal arts, and we set them the example."* The bishops were to organise parish primary schools run by their priests, and to improve the cathedral schools which would be of a secondary level similar to those of the monasteries. Many monasteries had two schools: one inner school for those intending to take vows and an outer school for potential lay priests or clerks in a secular life. The highest level of education was reserved for the Palace School in Aachen.

Alcuin's curriculum for the liberal arts was based on the ancient trivium and quadrivium of Greece which then passed to Rome. The trivium comprised grammar, rhetoric and dialectics and was the basic attainment at school level. Pupils could then proceed to studying arithmetic, geometry, music and astronomy if they were going to be deemed to have a good general education. Although pagan in origin, it was St Augustine who gave a legitimacy to studying these subjects as they were necessary to understand the Scriptures. And it was Boethius who had first used the terms trivium and quadrivium. The popular *Etymologies* of Isidore of Seville gave them further legitimacy. And so Alcuin reversed the influence of Jerome and helped to develop an early Christian humanism by claiming that the liberal arts were the work of God and that Christians should build on the work of the ancients.

During Charlemagne's time, the most effective of the schools were at the monasteries of Tours, Fulda, Auxerre, Ferrières, Reichenau, Corbie, St Gall, Rheims, Marmoutier, Fleury, Fontenelle, Bec and Cluny. Many of these schools had been in a poor state and Alcuin had to send for books from England and Rome. Generous gifts from rich families and the state meant that monks needed to rely less on their own subsistence farming. This attracted more educated monks. The renewal of these new schools in turn encouraged book production and the copying of books, both Christian and Classical writers, which helped preserve texts that might otherwise have been lost. Books produced in the Carolingian period were notably more literary than in previous centuries. In many cases only a single copy of a classical script had survived the Dark Ages. Like Cassiodorus three hundred years before, Alcuin praised the work of scribes and also wrote a treatise on orthography and tried to improve writing and punctuation. He encouraged the recently developed Carolingian (or Caroline) minuscule writing style which developed in the 780s.

Why was the Carolingian Renaissance important for saving the Classics?

The number of manuscripts in Europe is said to have increased from 2,000 in AD800 to 7,000 in AD 900. The new manuscripts were written in Caroline minuscule which blended Classical and Christian humanism. Those made at the abbey in Tours are regarded as the most beautiful examples. Alcuin also attracted scholars from throughout Europe to the court and many of these developed a curiosity about earlier Roman classical writers. It is known that at the St Gall monastery in the latter half of the tenth century, lectures were given on Cicero, Quintilian, Horace, Terence, Juvenal, Persius, Ovid and Sophocles.

Compared with the Greco-Roman achievements, or the Twelfth Century or the later Italian Renaissances, the Carolingian Renaissance is regarded as historically slight. Carolingian scholars did not research or create new knowledge, but they did reverse the cultural decay of the period since the fall of the Roman Empire. It was more a revival of the Latin language, Latin classical writers and Church fathers; it was about conserving rather than originating. But the increase in book production in the cathedrals and monasteries meant that no works of Roman classics that made it as far as 800 were lost between 800-1200. The importance of all this work is that our earliest known copies of many Roman literary texts date from the Carolingian period. And so in terms of the history of the book, the Carolingian Renaissance is very important.

After Charlemagne's death, his empire was attacked by Vikings, Saracens and Hungarians with monasteries sacked and regions devastated by war. The year 882 is when the court records end and could be said to mark the end of the Carolingian Renaissance. There was a brief continuation in Saxony where King Otto was less affected by invasion and war than was France and Italy and some German scholars refer to an Ottonian Renaissance to mark this period. It was short, and merely continued the work of Charlemagne. Although the monasteries and schools in Germany were not sacked and burned, there was no vitality associated with them.

However, the educational system established by Charlemagne and Alcuin in the cathedrals and monasteries survived as a faint glimmer in the darkness to await more propitious times. Alcuin had ensured that his pupils had been given influential positions as abbots and bishops to continue the work of bringing education to Europe and the trail led from Aachen to Tours, Fulda, Auxerre, Ferrières, Corbie, Reichenau, St Gall, Rheims and eventually Paris. This faint thread did not lead to the Twelfth Century Renaissance or the start of the University of Paris: that has to be attributed to the re-introduction of Greek genius via the Arabic intermediaries. In fact, the new universities with their focus on theology, law and medicine would force the Roman classics to retreat again until the Italian Renaissance in the fifteenth century .

But the cathedrals and monasteries had kept a teaching tradition alive and been centres for students which helped to make the forming of a university a more viable proposition. And Alcuin and his famous pupil, Rabanus Maurus (780-856), had made the seven liberal arts of the trivium and quadrivium the pattern that the universities would follow. These essentially pagan studies that had been questioned by earlier Christians were now found acceptable for a Christian education. The climax of Classical learning was probably between 1150-1200. Latin was to remain the language of scholarship until the late seventeenth century. It had obvious advantages: it was an international language; it was stable; and it allowed a high level of brevity, clarity and precision of meaning. It also bestowed on its users an aura of scholarship and exclusivity, which gave them a status and better justification for their higher fees and salaries.

Charlemagne had achieved the beginnings of what might be called a European civilisation. It blended the heritage of a Roman world empire; the intellectual achievements of Greece and Rome; a unified Latin Christianity; and the customs of the Germanic peoples. Europeans were becoming aware that their civilisation differed from the Byzantine and the Islamic civilisations so that this was the start of defining what was important for their future.

IV

THE ARABIC ROLE IN THE RECOVERY OF GREEK LEARNING

Were it not for the wisdom garnered in books, most of the learning would have been lost. The power of forgetfulness would have triumphed over the power of memory. **al-Jāḥiẓ (AD776-868)**

How well did the Greek classics survive in the Byzantine Empire?

As noted in the previous chapter, the Roman Emperor Constantine preferred to rule the empire from the East and built a new capital at Byzantium, an old Greek trading city on the Bosphorus. It was dedicated in AD330 and later renamed Constantinople. In AD395, the Roman Empire became formally split on the death of Theodosius between the Western part which looked to Rome, and the Eastern territories governed from Constantinople. After the split, the number of Latin speakers in the East declined. The Roman army kept the Latin tradition alive but, by the fifth century, it had declined to the point that Constantinople was in the hands of civilian palace officials and bureaucrats and the eastern Roman empire had become known as the Greek speaking Byzantine Empire. Unfortunately, the Byzantine empire never fulfilled the promise of its Hellenistic beginnings. No new scientific discoveries were made; no novel philosophical systems or explanations were forthcoming; no literary works entered world literature.

That said, the Byzantine Empire should have been well placed to ensure the survival of the Greek classics in the East. However, by the fifth and sixth centuries, Christian influence was strong and this was a time when church music, icons and mosaics were making the Greek classical writings look pagan and, therefore, unacceptable when the church was imposing Orthodox doctrine. During the reign of the Emperor Justinian (482-565), who wished to rule in a state that was completely Christian, teaching of the pagan classics was not permitted and many teachers were persecuted and books destroyed. Plato's original Academy in Athens was closed in 529. By this time learning and culture were in decline. Teaching of the literary classics began to focus on only a set number of texts, eg only seven plays by Sophocles and seven by Aeschylus were selected (and only these seven plays by each writer survive to this day). Inevitably, those not on the list were not copied as much, and for this reason have been lost to us. Besides, the emphasis was on Christian texts and not pagan Classics.

In addition, the crisis in the western Roman empire meant that Roman booksellers were not functioning effectively; papyrus was giving way to the more expensive parchment; the uncial script was large and wasteful ; and the shortage of slaves meant scribal costs had gone up. (Papyrus was lost to the West altogether with the Arab conquest of Egypt in 642). All this had the unfortunate effect that in the recopying of many papyrus documents on to parchment, the temptation was to shorten longer works into abridged versions or not to copy them at all. The minuscule script was first used in the Byzantine Empire probably in the late eighth century and the first dated example is in 835. Selected books in uncial were re-copied into minuscule, and it is from these that our knowledge of many Greek texts survives. The survival of papyri and uncial manuscripts is negligible.

Added to these problems were earthquakes and periodic uprisings and invasions. In 477 all 120,000 books in the imperial library were burnt in a local revolt. During the Byzantine "dark age" or Iconoclastic Crisis, from 727-843, Leo the Isaurian closed the imperial academy and its library of 36,000 books. Far worse was the Fourth Crusade. The taking of Constantinople in 1204 by the Crusaders was never their original intention or of Pope Innocent III who commissioned it: the Crusade was supposed to recapture Jerusalem. But after a series of mishaps, principally the animosity towards the Byzantines of the Doge of Venice, who provided the fleet of boats for the Crusaders; and the intrigue of a rival to the Byzantine emperor; the city was put under siege and then sacked over three days with a ferocity that could hardly have been worse. The most sophisticated Roman city then remaining, with possibly half a million inhabitants complete with aqueducts, baths, and libraries, was ransacked and many of its inhabitants raped and murdered. This is all the more surprising given that it was a Christian city, albeit a Greek Orthodox one and not a Roman Catholic one. Churches and monasteries were looted as any other building containing precious metal or jewels. Needless to say, books and manuscripts were not spared.

It was an elite of courtiers and bishops who kept up their interest in Plato, Sophocles, Euclid and Thucydides. Without them, many of the manuscripts which have passed down to us would have been lost and with them the small proportion of the Greek classics that we have. By the ninth century there was a renaissance of Byzantine learning with the imperial university revived. Students were taught the grammar of classical Greek, a literary language based on the educated speech of the fifth and fourth centuries BC, and markedly different from the Greek spoken in ninth century Byzantium. The school's graduates went on to become clerics or state dignitaries.

Leading figures in this were Leo the Armenian, Caesar Bardas and the Patriarch Photius.

The new dynasty of Basil I beginning in 867 was also conducive to scholarship. Arethas, who was archbishop of Caesarea from 903, was a classical scholar who wrote commentaries on Plato and Lucian. He also bought the Euclid manuscript in 888 that is now in the Bodleian. This brief flourishing of learning continued under Constantine Porphyrogenitus, who died in 959, but relapsed until Constantine IX Monomachos came to the throne in 1042. In his reign the Greek classics flourished and so did the book trade making many more copies which found their way to the libraries and cultural centres throughout the empire. It was this decentralisation that allowed copies of the classics to survive the Fourth Crusade. The Byzantines reconquered Constantinople in 1261 and the city remained the capital until 1453 when it fell to the Ottoman Turks.

Despite these minor renaissances, many works were lost. The Bibliotheca of Patriarch Photius (c.820–893) comprises 279 book reviews. Some 80 of the books reviewed have disappeared. And in the tenth century, another Byzantine encyclopaedia of 30,000 entries called the Suda was compiled. Such compilations kept alive an awareness of Greek classical writers for future humanists, as well as increasing the frustration when assessing the losses from the Greek heritage.

Why did Greek texts get translated in to Syriac?

Greek was not widely spoken in the eastern parts of the Byzantine Empire such as Syria and Iraq. The local language was Syriac, a dialect of Aramaic, and was certainly the language of the Christians. Greek remained the language of Christians in the parts of the empire bordering the Mediterranean Sea (although in Egypt the main language was Coptic, a descendant of ancient Egyptian).

To facilitate teaching, translations of Greek texts were made in Syriac for those living in the Middle East. These were Hellenistic rather than Hellenic: in other words, scientific, medical and philosophical texts rather than the works of earlier poets, dramatists, orators and historians which were not of interest. In some cases, the original Greek has been lost and only a Syriac translation exists, eg the *Meteorology* of Theophrastus, some works by Archimedes and Hero of Alexandria.

There were intellectual centres, one of the earliest being at Nisibis, a frontier town with a large Jewish population on the road from Mesopotamia to Damascus. After the Council of Nicaea in 325, the original Jewish academy at Nisibis , which had suffered under the Romans, became a Christian academy. This was followed by another Christian centre at Edessa after the Persians retook, in 363, land ceded to the Romans. Some translation from Greek to Syriac took place at Edessa, works by Aristotle and Porphyry among them.

The next major development was the Nestorian schism. Nestorius (c386-450) became Archbishop of Constantinople. This was a time when there were rivalries between church factions in Antioch and Alexandria with differing views on when the soul enters the body and the impact this had on the veneration of the Virgin Mary as the bearer of the divine Son of God. In supporting the losing Antioch faction, Nestorius found himself deprived of his position and was excommunicated in 431. The school of Edessa had supported Nestorius and so found itself branded Nestorian. And to avoid further hostility, the school closed in 489 and moved east to Nisibis where it found more favour with the Persian rulers and became the centre of Nestorian Christianity. As well as the doctrinal schism, by moving eastward, the Nestorians became more Persian and links with the Greek orthodoxy of Constantinople weakened, for example, clergy could marry.

What influence did the Nestorians have?

The Nestorians spread Christianity through parts of Arabia, India and China and remained independent of Rome until 1804. In Persia, they found great favour under the Sasanian king Khosrow I (531–578). In the mid sixth century, Khosrow gave shelter to Greek scholars and Nestorian Christians fleeing persecution from Justinian in the Byzantine empire. This was a time when the Academy had been closed in Athens and the scholarly Khosrow had a vision of setting up a Persian version of it.

The school of Nisibis continued but mainly as a theological college. Khosrow allowed the Byzantine refugees to set up what many scholars regard as an early university specialising in medicine, astronomy and philosophy at Gondishapur (its ruins are near Shahabad in Iran). It had a hospital and trained doctors with Greek medical knowledge. Moreover, scholars were invited from China and India which brought knowledge of herbal medicine; both countries having contacts through either the Nestorian Christian networks or the Persians. The Persian Sasanian dynasty had maintained diplomatic and trade ties with China along the Silk Road. The Sasanians had also imported books from India which brought mathematics, astronomy and astrology.

As well as medical training, Gondishapur followed the Alexandrian model desired by Khosrow and had an observatory and faculty of astronomy, with mathematics as subsidiary to that. Teaching was in Syriac, and many more translations from Greek to Syriac were made at Gondishapur than had been done previously at Edessa. It was mainly through the school at Gondishapur that Greek knowledge first passed to the Arabs, filtered through translations into Syriac.

When were the Arab conquests?

The Prophet Muhammad died in 632. During his last years, the Arabs occupied what is now Saudi Arabia and Yemen. Within two years of his death, successors in Medina decided on a bold expansionist policy to take more territory which would include Jerusalem. The opposing forces would comprise the Byzantine and the Sasanian, or Persian, empires.

Within four years, in 636, the Byzantines had been beaten at the Battle of Yarmouk in Palestine. The defeat at Yarmouk, just east of the Sea of Galilee, enabled the Muslim Arabs to take Jerusalem, Antioch and Aleppo from the Byzantines. This was an extraordinary accomplishment given that the Arabs were a ragged and not especially well equipped force. But they were seasoned horsemen, well co-ordinated, and highly motivated with new religious zeal. The desert and steppe landscapes were ideal for their fast moving cavalry. Another battle in 636 saw the Sasanians defeated at Qadisiyyah on the banks of the Euphrates which gave the Arabs access to all of Iraq. And between 639 and 642 they took the whole of Byzantine Egypt including Alexandria.

Who were the Umayyads?

There then followed rivalry between Arab factions as to who would become leader and take the successes further. Eventually Al Mu'awiyah became caliph in 661 and he moved the capital from Medina to Damascus and founded the Umayyad dynasty, named after the clan to which his family belonged, the Banu Umayyah. He made further conquests in central Asia but was unable to take Constantinople despite the Arabs developing an effective navy.

Within 40 years from the Prophet's death, the Arabs had an empire stretching from Portugal to the borders of China. Arabic began to replace the Byzantine Greek and the Sasanian Pahlavi languages. And the conquests of north Africa added to the empire with Carthage falling in 697. Spain was invaded in 711 and almost the entire Iberian peninsula taken from the Visigoths. The furthest extent reached in Europe was north-west France where the Arabs were finally halted by Charles Martel at the Battle of Tours in 732.

The Umayyad dynasty was based in Syria. It lasted until 750. Although the Umayyads had a passion for architectural projects, eg the Dome of the Rock in Jerusalem, the relentless appetite for increasing territory left little time for culture and learning. Islam was never a religion of enforced conversion. The Arabs were content to leave Jews and Christians to practise their own religion and to carry out their lives much as they always had. Islamic law guaranteed toleration for Christians and Jews as "Peoples of the Book", peoples to whom God had granted a partial revelation, reserving the fullness of it for his Prophet Muḥammad. The condition was that they had to pay a tax, the jizyah, which was paid by all non-Muslims as the price for protection within the Islamic state. Effectively, the Arabs found that life after conquest was made much easier by extracting taxes from doing nothing other than letting people get on with their lives. However, the official language of government in Damascus changed from Greek to Arabic in 799.

During the ninety years of the Umayyad dynasty they were faced with internal conflict, much of it from Kufa in Iraq, the main power centre of the Shī'a Muslims, supporters of the Prophet's nephew ʿAlī (Shīʿat ʿAlī means 'party of ʿAlī'), who they thought should have succeeded him as leader, and also from the Persian region of Khurasan where descendants of the Prophet's uncle al-ʿAbbās, who would later inaugurate the ʿAbbāsid dynasty, were laying claim to power. The supporters of the family of al-ʿAbbās were aided by the resentment built up against the Umayyads who only allowed Arabs to hold positions of power, not anyone of foreign descent. The Muslim converts were thus unable to achieve advancement despite many of them coming from what they regarded as a superior Persian civilisation. The local feeling was very much against what many saw as people of inferior culture.

Who were the 'Abbāsids?

The 'Abbāsids take their name from al-'Abbās (566-653) who was the uncle of the Prophet. Their overthrow of the Umayyads was particularly bloodthirsty. The 'Abbāsid leader invited all the Umayyad family to a conciliatory dinner in Damascus where he had them killed. As well as being unpopular with the local population, stricter Muslims found the Umayyads rather too loose in their interpretation of Islam. The Umayyads saw themselves as Arabs first and Muslims second, which did not go down too well with true believers. The one survivor from the family massacre was a young prince named 'Abd al-Raḥmān who escaped to Spain and continued the Umayyad dynasty in Córdoba for a further three centuries.

The 'Abbāsids promoted themselves as upholders of Islam above everything else. They appealed to many new converts to Islam as they did not see that being an Arab was an essential prerequisite for holding any position of power. They moved the capital from Damascus in Syria to Baghdad in Iraq, a completely new city they founded in 762.

Why move the capital of the caliphate to Baghdad?

The site of Baghdad was chosen by the 'Abbāsid caliph Al-Manṣūr (714-775) who had taken over the caliphate on the death of his brother. The move eastward to an area in the heart of the former Sasanian empire was nearer their power base in Khurasan, and also in part a way of paying back the assistance that the Persians had shown to the 'Abbāsids in their overthrow of the Umayyads. Baghdad was only some 25 miles from the old Sasanian capital of Ctesiphon. Al-Manṣūr had made a close friendship with a leading Persian family, the Barmakids from the city of Merv on the Silk Road, who had been especially supportive. They were sophisticated, familiar with the Greek classics, and had an interesting background having been Buddhists from Afghanistan.

The land around the new capital in Mesopotamia, conveniently situated between the Rivers Tigris and Euphrates, was also particularly fertile and at times allowed three crops a year. Its fertility had previously seen the Sumerian, Babylonian, and Assyrian civilisations flourish in the same area.

Within 50 years, Baghdad had a population of half a million, comprising Arabs, Persians, Turks, Bedouins, Africans, Greeks, Jews, Indians, and Slavs. Many were slaves. Like Alexandria, built in 323BC, it was a new city that would become a major centre of culture and learning.

Why were the 'Abbāsids supporters of learning?

The 'Abbāsids were fascinated by Persian culture, in a similar way to the earlier Roman admiration for Greek culture. In fact, to make a similar observation to that made by Horace, while the Arabs conquered Persia militarily and politically, the artistic and intellectual conquest belonged to the Persians. Although they were Arabs, speaking Arabic and with religion that had originated in the peninsula of Arabia, many caliphs had strong Persian links by marriage and education. They appointed more Persians than Arabs as chief ministers.

The 'Abbāsids were keen to avail themselves of this more advanced knowledge which was to be found not just in Gondishapur. Educating the officials needed to administer their vast empire was a main driver of this need to acquire knowledge. Many of the centres that had been nurtured by Alexander the Great such as Merv, Aleppo, Heliopolis (Baalbek), and Alexandria, had retained Greek scholarship and all were now in territory controlled by the 'Abbāsids. In addition, their capital was in the middle of a region where Nestorian Christianity was strongest. There were churches and monasteries in and near the new city, and the Nestorian patriarch was established nearby. The learning preserved in Nestorian libraries and developed by Nestorian scholars became available to the new Muslim rulers.

Only three years after founding Baghdad, al-Manṣūr was taken seriously ill with a gastric disorder. The advice was to send for the head of the hospital and academy at Gondishapur, a Nestorian called Jirjis ibn Bukhtishu, who stayed on as the court physician and helped cement the link with Gondishapur. With support from the Barmakids, a steady stream of academics were attracted to Baghdad from Gondishapur which was about 300 miles away.

What was the Translation Movement?

The intellectual and religious openness of the 'Abbāsids allowed Christians, Jews, and Persians to move to Baghdad which became what we would call a multicultural society. Many non-Muslims were given posts in government of high responsibility, given that they had talents and skills that the 'Abbāsids did not yet have. However, al-Manṣūr did not want non-Muslims to develop too much influence by their superior knowledge. Having founded a library in 762 for all the books he was accumulating in Pahlavi, Sanskrit, Coptic, Greek and Syriac, he embarked on a state sponsored translation project so that the books were translated into Arabic. The 'Abbāsids also had an underlying insecurity about maintaining themselves in power. Having overthrown the Umayyads, al-Manṣūr was keen to govern well and he felt there would be lessons from the books of other cultures that could give guidance.

The subjects covered at first were principally practical ones such as astronomy and mathematics. Astronomy was particularly important for worship: calculating the sacred direction of Mecca and placing the mihrab in a mosque to mark the direction in which worshippers faced during prayer; and for calculating the dates of the sighting of the moon. The stars had also played a large role in Zoroastrianism, the Persian religion. Soon, the emphasis was finding original Greek texts as it became apparent that many Persian texts were later translations of the Greek. (This caused some affront to the Persians who claimed that the works were originally Persian but had been appropriated by Alexander the Great in his conquests!). At a later stage medicine was translated. Philosophy was then included, primarily as the Arabs felt at a disadvantage when discussing subjects with Christians and Jews who had a better grounding in reasoning and debating. Greek poetry and drama were never of interest as literary and cultural influences came from Arab culture as well as from Persia. But the Indian contribution to mathematics was recognised as also the Persian astronomical observations.

The movement (although it was more the practical outcome of a general interest in intellectual matters, with little detailed central planning) was greatly aided by the arrival of paper. The Arabs had defeated a Chinese army north-west of Samarkand in 751. Among the Chinese prisoners brought to Samarkand were men who knew how to make paper. A paper mill was set up in Samarkand using local flax and hemp instead of the mulberry bark used by the Chinese. The first paper mill in Baghdad appeared in 793 allowing much cheaper material for book production than papyrus or parchment.

The House of Wisdom

Al-Manṣūr's grandson, Hārūn Al-Rashīd (763-809), continued the quest for books to be translated and sent people far and wide in the search, even raiding parties in to the Byzantine empire. It was he who founded the Bayt al-Ḥikmah, or House of Wisdom, as a library to house the books and the scholars, among whom Nestorian Christians were prominent, to translate them. Baghdad became home to many private libraries as well, with scholarship valued by the rich and powerful.

Hārūn's death led to a power struggle for succession between his sons. Al-Ma'mūn (786-833) became caliph in 813 and he was probably the most scholarly of the early caliphs. He continued the quest for books and by the mid-ninth century, the House of Wisdom was the largest library in the world. Rather like Gondishapur, the peace and harmony in Baghdad attracted scholars from afar and works were translated not just from Greek, Syriac and Persian, but from Sanskrit and Chinese.

Does this mean that all the Arabs accomplished was a translation of Greek knowledge into Arabic?

The wealth of books from different languages aided the task of the translators. Instead of simply translating word for word, good translators, with a knowledge of several languages, could compare texts and work out the meaning of each sentence. They would have to be competent subject specialists to do this and the best translators were already eminent scientists or doctors.

The assembly of scholars in Baghdad under the patronage of the caliphs were certainly learning from the translations being made but were also building on them by creating new knowledge. At its simplest, just co-ordinating works by Greek and Indian mathematicians and scientists gave them the chance to make new connections. The Translation Movement itself came to an end in the latter half of the tenth century. By that time, some 200 years in all, the necessary translation had been completed and Islamic science and medicine had developed its own momentum. Islamic scientists were now improving on the wisdom they had absorbed. Perhaps a few examples would be helpful:

Ḥunayn ibn Isḥāq (809-73) was a Christian fluent in Syriac, Greek and Arabic who had trained as a doctor at Gondishapur. He and his team would create technical vocabulary in Arabic and then cross-check each other's work. Amongst Ḥunayn and his team's accomplishments were that they translated 129 works by the Greek medical writer Galen; works by Hippocrates; Republic, Laws and Timaeus of Plato; mathematical works of Euclid and Archimedes; and logical works of Aristotle. The combination of Ḥunayn 's subject specialism and the ability to cross check versions from several different languages within his team meant that their translated texts formed a gold standard.

In addition, Ḥunayn was the court physician to al al-Ma'mūn. He also wrote the first systematic textbook on opthalmology.

The **Banū Mūsā** brothers were commissioned by al-Ma'mūn to measure the circumference of the earth. They were accomplished engineers and mathematicians and knew the work of Ptolemy. They walked in to the desert at night in different directions and, using the stars, travelled until the furthest north and furthest south brother had measured a one degree angle of the earth's curve. Measuring the distance between them and multiplying by 360 gave them a circumference of 24,500 miles, only 400 miles less than the figure given by modern science. (That said, Eratosthenes in Alexandria came up with a figure of 25,000 miles in 240BC, but he was only a librarian).

Muhammad ibn Mūsā al-Khwarizmī (780-850) was the person who made the Hindu/Arabic numeral system the standard the world has used since. He also effectively invented algebra and trigonometry through his development of quadratic equations, sine, cosine and tangent tables. He made major contributions to astronomy and geography and was also the Librarian of the House of Wisdom.

Al-Kindī (801-873) is best known as the father of Arab philosophy through his work to make Aristotle and the Neoplatonists accessible and acceptable to Islam. He wrote some 260 books which ranged in subjects from geometry to medicine, philosophy, logic, optics, chemistry, music, meteorology and physics. And he was one of the earliest cryptographers. **Al-Fārābī** (d.950) built on the thinking of Al-Kindī by developing a system of Aristotelian and neo-Platonic philosophy acceptable to Islam.

Muhammad ibn Zakariyā al-Rāzī (854-925), or Rhazes as he is known in Europe, was an eminent doctor developing clinical experiments with control groups. Medicine in Baghdad was quite sophisticated as they had employed doctors and borrowed best practice from the university and teaching hospital in Gondishapur. A hospital was founded as early as 800 in Baghdad and others in the provinces followed. One of Rhazes' books helped distinguish between measles and smallpox, and he made major contributions to paediatrics and psychology. He also began to compile an enormous medical encyclopedia in which he gave the views of previous writers who had written in Greek, Syriac, Persian, Indian and Arabic, and then gave his own views based on clinical observation. He also made contributions to chemistry and alchemy including a rudimentary periodic table.

Ibn al-Haytham or **Alhazen** (965-1040) is best known for his *Book of Optics*. He had studied Euclid and Aristotle's views on how the eye sees objects but did not agree with their classical model of a cone of light projecting from the eye. He reversed Aristotle's theory and showed that light travels in straight lines and reflects from an object to the eyes. He also worked out that it is the brain that processes what is seen rather than the eyes. His experiments made discoveries in refraction of light when it passes through a fluid, and he also made pioneering insights into binocular vision which made development of eyeglasses possible in the thirteenth century .

Ibn al-Haytham was probably the first scientist to use modern scientific method as he gave details of his methods and mathematical proofs which allowed all his work to be checked or replicated by other scientists, eg his estimate of the thickness of the earth's atmosphere (which was out by 50%). He also made contributions to mathematics. The impact crater on the moon named Alhazen honours his contribution to astronomy.

Two other great figures of the Islamic Golden Age worked outside the main centre in Baghdad. **Abū ʿAlī al-Ḥusayn ibn ʿAbdillāh ibn al-Ḥasan ibn ʿAlī ibn Sīnā**, better known as **Avicenna** (980-1037), was a Persian polymath born near Bukhārā. He became a physician at the age of eighteen and is best known in the West for his medical writing. Much of his life was spent travelling with patrons in modern day Persia, although he settled in Isfahan for a time. Of the 240 surviving texts that he wrote, some 40 works are on medical subjects, of which the *Canon of Medicine*, a medical encyclopaedia, is the best known. This is a five volume summation of the writing of Greek, Indian, Chinese and Arabic medical discovery and practice and was in use in Europe until the seventeenth century, principally for its clarity and organisation. Avicenna explained contagious diseases; sexually transmitted diseases; introduced quarantine to limit the spread of infectious diseases; organised clinical trials; and introduced the idea of a syndrome in the diagnosis of specific diseases.

There are also 150 other works on philosophical and religious topics of which *The Book of Healing* is the most famous. This book is intended to cure or heal ignorance of the soul. It covers many scientific subjects but is known for its reconciling of Aristotle and Islamic doctrine. He also wrote on many other subjects including astronomy, astrology, physics, chemistry, geology and psychology.

Abū l-Walīd Muḥammad ibn 'Aḥmad Ibn Rushd, better known as **Averroës** (1126–98), was born in Córdoba and was another polymath. Much of his working life was spent as a judge, but he was also a court physician to the Almohad Caliphate. He wrote some 100 books covering law, medicine, philosophy, astronomy, physics, and psychology. However, he is best known for his extensive commentaries on Aristotle. Averroës felt that writers such as Avicenna and Al-Fārābī had misinterpreted Aristotle. His commentaries on Aristotle reached western Europe in the thirteenth century at a time when not all of Aristotle had been translated from the original Greek. His importance on western thinking during the Scholastic period is such that he is referred to as "The Commentator" on Aristotle. His work was used both to clarify Aristotle's writing and to give detailed, line by line, commentary.

Jim al Khalili's book on The House of Wisdom gives many more examples of the men involved in Islamic scientific advances during this period. He shows that the House of Wisdom was very similar to the Museion at the Library of Alexandria in being not just a library but a research institute and academy as well. And by bringing together scientists from across the world to discuss previous work and the discrepancies they revealed, eg astronomical tables, this is perhaps the first time that scientists had worked together on cross disciplinary problems in the way that we are familiar with today.

The accomplishments of the Islamic Golden Age can be seen in a book compiled by the mid-tenth century writer Isḥāq al-Nadīm. *The Al-Fihrist* is a compendium that is part biography and part bibliography, rather like the *Pinakes* compiled by Callimachus in the Library of Alexandria. It references 10,000 books and 3,500 authors in roughly chronological order. All the books are in Arabic and the subject range is vast. It gives a good snapshot of what existed in the libraries of Baghdad at its publication in 938.

It is as well to also appreciate the quality of Islamic manuscripts. The Greeks and Romans had never produced elaborate scripts as their books were utilitarian, although collectors had beautified the outside of their papyrus rolls. The Christian west had produced some amazingly beautiful manuscript books such as the *Book of Kells* and *The Lindisfarne Gospels*, but these were rare and designated for a very small elite. Islamic calligraphers, by contrast, made the book itself a thing of beauty and the feel and look of a book as well as the writing was valued. Many elaborate binding techniques were later imported into western European practice.

After the tenth century, the 'Abbāsid rule became troubled by conflicts. Eventually, Baghdad was sacked in 1258 by a Mongol army under the command of Genghis Khan's grandson. Many of the books were destroyed except those on astronomy and alchemy. The Golden Age had also seen libraries and intellectual centres in Basra, Mosul, Cairo, Damascus, Kufa, Aleppo, Bukhārā, Shiraz and Tripoli so that survival was higher than if all had been centralised in Baghdad.

Did the ʿAbbāsids conquer Spain?

The North African Berbers invaded Spain via Gibraltar in 711. The name Gibraltar comes from the Muslim leader Jabal Tariq (Mount Tariq) who led the invasion. The Romans had colonised Spain many years before and it had benefited from their agricultural innovation, and the development of a number of well developed urban centres. But the Vandal invasions in 409 completed the collapse of the Roman occupation of Iberia. Another German tribe, the Visigoths, took over their territorial gains soon after that, leading to two centuries of stagnation and urban depopulation as in most of the rest of western Europe.

The Muslims captured most of Iberia quite quickly except for the far north which remained Christian. (The word Spain will be used hereafter as most of the events described were in the area now known as Spain. However, the Arabs occupied the land that we know as Portugal as well, evidenced by names such as Algarve, Alentejo and Alfama). The Romans had made Córdoba a regional capital in 152BC and built the bridge over the River Guadalquivir. Both the elder and younger Seneca were born in Córdoba. It was, therefore, an obvious place for the Muslims to take on as their regional capital for the south of Spain, the country which became known to them as al-Andalus from as early as 715.

The first few decades of Muslim rule were not very stable with new waves of tribesmen entering from north Africa and vying for ascendancy. There was an obvious need for strong leadership to pull the new territory together. It was noted above that when the ʿAbbāsids slaughtered the Umayyad leaders in Damascus in 750, one prince escaped. ʿAbd al-Raḥmān (731-788) fled to north Africa and eventually reached Spain in 755 landing in Almuñécar. He formed an army with Spanish Muslims sympathetic to the Umayyads. After he had established himself, including the peaceful fall of Seville, he settled in Córdoba. There he set up an Umayyad emirate becoming Emir ʿAbd al-Raḥmān I.

When did Córdoba become a centre for Arabic learning?

'Abd al-Raḥmān I encouraged improvements in agriculture using irrigation techniques borrowed from drier countries under Islamic control and reviving the canals built by the Romans. His great grandson and the fourth emir was 'Abd al-Raḥmān II who ruled from 822–852. He benefited from the wealth brought by these agricultural developments and began seriously trading with Mediterranean and Middle Eastern countries. The traders and pilgrims to Mecca on the Hajj brought awareness of the scholarship in Baghdad, which encouraged Córdoba to develop its own centres of learning. The Jewish population thrived under the Umayyads after a period of persecution by the Visigoths and they were often well educated – some 50% of all doctors in Iberia at this period were Jewish.

Books began to arrive from Baghdad, Cairo, Timbuktu and Fez. A royal library was established in the 850s. It was under Raḥmān III who ruled from 912–961 that Córdoba entered its golden age of scholarship. Raḥmān III's court attracted scholars from all over Iberia and beyond, and became a centre for the study of medicine, astronomy, canon law, grammar and poetry. Córdoba grew to a city of almost 100,000 people; larger than Paris, Rome and London combined and almost the size of Constantinople. The city became famed for its craftsmen and luxury goods. No longer feeling inferior to Baghdad, 'Abd al-Raḥmān III declared it a caliphate in 929.

His son, al-Ḥakam II, was probably more enthusiastic about learning than his father and combined three royal libraries into one said to contain 400,000 books and employ 500 staff. The librarian, Talid, made a title catalogue filling 404 volumes. All books needed copying to preserve them and scribes in Córdoba wrote 70,000 to 80,000 books a year.

What did Córdoba contribute to scholarship?

By this time, little translation was left to do from Greek which was a good thing as no-one in Córdoba knew any Greek. When, in 949, the Byzantine Emperor Constantine VII sent a copy of the *De Materia Medica*, the famous herbal by Dioscorides with painted pictures of the plants, there was great excitement. But the Caliph had to request the Emperor to send someone who could translate it. The monk sent, Nicolas, duly did so and the translation was better than the one made in Baghdad by Ḥunayn ibn Isḥāq. The translation of this book helped to generate a focus on medicine in Córdoba.

The most eminent of the new generation of doctors was the court physician to al-Ḥakam II, **'Abbās al-Zahrāwī** (936-1013) who is better known by his Latin name **Albucasis**. He wrote a medical compendium, Kitāb al-taṣrīf, or the *Method of Medicine*, that was to be used throughout the middle ages alongside Avicenna's *Canon*. He is best known for his design of surgical instruments as well as pioneering catgut for stitching and opium as an anaesthetic.

One of the earliest Andalusian polymaths, **'Abbās ibn Firnās** (809-887) from Ronda, brought copies of al-Khwarizmī's mathematical works and developed Andalusian astronomy in the mid-ninth century.

In the twelfth century two great thinkers were born there: Maimonides (c.1135-1204) who was a Jewish philosopher; and Ibn Rushd, or Averroës (1126-98), who was noted above as the great Commentator on Aristotle. The geographer, al-Idrīsī, studied here before joining the court of King Roger in Sicily where he produced a world map used for centuries after.

When did the golden age in Córdoba end?

Al-Ḥakam II died in 976. Shortly afterwards his vizier, al-Manṣūr, took over. Al-Manṣūr had more religious fundamentalist beliefs and began to destroy all scientific books as he felt that these were not known to their ancestors and so were heretical. Some of the books saved were scattered and scholars took them to other Iberian centres such as Granada, Seville, Zaragoza, and Toledo. The royal palace was dismantled to be sold off for profit.

Al-Manṣūr had invited Berber Arabs from north Africa to support his takeover. When he died in 1002, he was succeeded by his son who died in 1008. With no obvious successor, a power struggle ensued and the Berbers sensed an opportunity. They laid siege to Córdoba from 1010–13 during which many books from the libraries were auctioned off to provide funds for essentials. The caliphate finally came to an end in 1031 and was replaced by warlords running taifas or city states. When the Christian north began raiding the warlords, the remaining Muslims asked their Berber brethren in north Africa for help. The Almoravids obliged and were in power from 1085–1145. They were more fundamentalist than the Umayyads and libraries were not well supported. The Almoravids were in turn overthrown by the Almohads, also from north Africa, who ruled from 1172 to 1223.

The caliphate of Córdoba had been one of the richest and most powerful states in Europe. Eventually the Christians under King Ferdinand III of Castile reclaimed Córdoba in 1236. La Mezquita, the mosque commissioned by 'Abd al-Raḥmān I in 784, was turned in to a cathedral and remains one of the most extraordinary sacred spaces in Europe combining Moorish arches with Gothic additions. The fall of the Islamic al-Andalus finally came with the Christians taking Granada in 1492. In 1499, Cardinal Ximénez de Cisneros burned all Islamic books in an attempt to erase the Islamic past in Spain.

Why did Islam lose this lead in science?

By the twelfth century, the scientists in Baghdad, Córdoba and other centres were way ahead of any in Europe. There is some truth in the view that Islamic science was dependent on earlier Greek authorities, as well as Indian mathematics, and so their work could be said to be an extended commentary and development of earlier models rather than truly original. However, the sheer depth and vitality of Islamic science at a time when western Europe was putting its energy in to matters like canon law and Biblical interpretation, was impressive. As to why this should be, one theory is that having completed their conquests of land, they had turned to asserting the superiority of Islam by achieving a conquest of the mind, absorbing all the known wisdom of the world they had conquered. Islamic science was to act as a bridge between the Classical world and early western science.

But the Twelfth Century Renaissance and then the Enlightenment of the sixteenth and seventeenth centuries saw the work of Vesalius, Copernicus, Fuchs, Newton, etc put European scientists in the forefront of advances in science and medicine. Not a lot stirred in Islamic science during this time.

There are several explanations as to why Islam lost its lead. There was a twelfth century conservative reaction against Greek philosophical ideas and a feeling that science was straying from true Islam. The fall of Baghdad to Mongol invaders in 1258 was certainly another blow, and there was the Reconquista in Spain and the Crusades all happening at the same time. There is also the rejection of printing. Islam had always valued the relation of tutor to pupil and the ability to authenticate any writing done by the pupil which needed to be in manuscript. The printing press was seen as a threat to this relationship. Printing in Arabic in any Muslim country only began in 1727, in Turkey, some three hundred years after Gutenberg's invention. Printing in Arabic was certainly difficult, as with Chinese and Japanese characters, but books in Arabic had appeared in Italy as early as 1514.

And after the discovery of the Americas in 1492, power was shifting westwards and with it the wealth needed to support science. The traditional trade routes were losing their importance in the Middle

East. Although the Twelfth Century Renaissance recognised the importance of Islamic science, by the Italian Renaissance it had largely been written out of the western consciousness. Even today the names of great western scientists from the sixteenth, seventeenth and eighteenth centuries are well known but hardly anyone could name any of the great Islamic scientists from the Golden Age.

When and how did Greek/Arabic knowledge filter to northern Europe?

There would always have been diplomatic and trading contacts between the Islamic and Christian countries with some awareness that the Islamic countries were more advanced in scientific knowledge. But few northern Europeans spoke Arabic or Greek. Latin was the language of scholars, many of whom were monks working in monastery libraries or attached to the courts of powerful monarchs. One of the earliest known contacts with Arabic learning was Gerbert d'Aurillac (c945-1003), a French monk who studied some of the translations that had found their way to the monastery at Vic in Catalonia. Through these he achieved a mastery of mathematics and astronomy that was in advance of any other scholar in western Europe. He was made Abbot of Bobbio and then head of the cathedral school at Rheims which became an intellectual centre along with Chartres. He is thought to have written the first Latin text on the astrolabe as well as building sundials and designing musical organs. He also brought awareness of the Arabic (or Indian) numeral system, although the system did not become widely used for another two centuries as we will shortly see. In the year 999 he was elected pope, taking the name Sylvester II, and had ambitions to revive the Carolingian Renaissance, but died only four years into his papacy. However, he foreshadowed many of the advances in European thought that were to follow.

Gerbert had paved the way for the main transmission route to the north through Spain. As the Christians began to reconquer more territory in al-Andalus from the Muslims, more Islamic texts became available for translators. A parallel source was through Sicily, which was reconquered in 1091 by the Normans, and to a lesser extent medicine through the city of Salerno. The exceptions to these well trodden paths were isolated travellers such as Adelard of Bath and Leonardo Fibonacci.

Adelard of Bath

Adelard (c.1080–c1152) is believed to have been born in Bath. He is known to have died there and been in the community of Benedictine monks at Bath Abbey. It is thought that Bishop John of Villula, who moved the bishopric from Wells to Bath in 1090, encouraged him to study in Tours. From there he taught mathematics at the cathedral school in Laon and then travelled for seven years through Greece, Sicily, Syria and Palestine becoming especially interested in Arabic mathematics and astronomy. He learnt Arabic and translated the astronomical tables, or zij, of al-Khwarizmī which introduced algebra into Europe, and made the first full translation of Euclid's *Elements* into Latin. This gave scholars in Europe the complete basics of geometry instead of the abbreviated version handed down from Boethius. Adelard also wrote a textbook on the abacus; a guide to the astrolabe; a work entitled *Questiones Naturales* which was a summary of what he had learnt from the Arabs; and a treatise on falconry.

Adelard's writing influenced two of the men who made science important at the recently founded Oxford University: Robert Grosseteste (1175–1253) and Roger Bacon (c.1219–1292). Modern science begins in thirteenth century Europe based on the translations from Greek and Arabic.

Fibonacci

Leonardo Fibonacci (c1170–1240) came from Pisa and travelled in Sicily, Algeria, Egypt and Syria. His father was the head of the Pisan trading colony at Bougie in Algeria and would have realised the superiority of the Arabic numerals over the Roman numerals when it came to trade. In these countries they observed the use of Arabic numerals for commercial calculations such as money conversion, and calculating profit and interest rates. Although Gerbert had become familiar with this system some 200 years earlier, it was Fibonacci's book *Liber Abbaci*, published in 1202, that explained its role in problem solving and that popularised it. He is remembered mainly for being the first to describe the Fibonacci sequence 1,2,3,5,8,13,21,34 etc where each number is the sum of the two preceding numbers.

With this book, the words zero and cipher also entered the western vocabulary. Islam had already given the word algebra from mathematics, and from astronomy the words almanac, zenith, nadir and azimuth.

The Crusades

The First Crusade began in 1096 and the Crusades lasted until 1492. Whilst the Crusaders were noble in their aims, they were soldiers and admiring Islamic scholarship would not have been high on their list of the spoils of conquest. In fact, destruction of libraries when cities were conquered hindered the transfer of knowledge. The worst example being the Fourth Crusade which saw the destruction of much of Constantinople in 1204, a certain own goal as it was a Christian city belonging to the eastern Roman empire.

Crusaders were also involved in the Reconquista of Spain. And it was the capture of cities like Toledo and later centres in al-Andalus that gave access to the treasures of the Islamic libraries.

Translations from Arabic into Latin in Spain

It was noted above that many documents were scattered after the fall of the Córdoban caliphate. The main centre for their reception was Toledo which became Christian again in 1085. Fortunately, the transition from the Muslims was peaceful and the libraries in Toledo remained even though their owners went further south. It must be remembered that the largest monastic library in western Europe at this time contained perhaps 700 books, so that scholars from the north were amazed at the size of the Muslim libraries. The royal library alone in Córdoba was known to have had 400,000 books, albeit scrolls that would not contain as much text as a codex.

One difficulty facing the translators, apart from selection, was whether to translate the Greek original or to include the many Arabic glosses that had been added by scholars in Baghdad and Córdoba. The answer in some cases was easy: the *Canon* of Avicenna was in 5 volumes and was an excellent summary and restructuring of the rambling works of Galen which had occupied 500 treatises and some 10 million words. (The Galenic corpus that has come down to us is 3 million words and forms about half of the surviving literature from ancient Greece!). A second difficulty was then that the vocabulary in Latin had to be created as many of the concepts and methodologies used in Arabic advances in science were unknown in Europe.

During the twelfth century, the main patron for the translators was Raymond, who was archbishop of the cathedral of Toledo from 1125 to 1151. He gave his blessings to many foreigners who came to learn from the riches of Greek and Arabic learning now available. It was really only in the twelfth century that European scholars interested in philosophy and science realised how much they had to learn from the Arabs. Gerard of Cremona (c1114-1187) was the most important of the Toledo translators and was made a canon of the cathedral. He studied astronomy and he travelled to Toledo as he had hoped to find there a copy of Ptolemy's *Almagest*. He translated, together with assistants, between 70 and 100 scientific works from Arabic which included Aristotle, Euclid, Archimedes, Ptolemy and Galen and also the works of al-Khwarizmī, al-Kindī, al-Rāzī, Ibn Sīnā, and others. The Toledo translation school in many ways resembled that of the House of Wisdom in Baghdad some 300 years earlier. Gerard learned Arabic, but many of the translators worked in a multilingual environment with Jews, Mozarabs (Christians who had learned Arabic), and the locals speaking a Romance language. The Toledo school of translators tended to make literal, word by word translations.

During the twelfth century, the translation of Euclid transformed geometry. The most influential translation was that of Adelard of Bath, but there was another by Gerard of Cremona and a third by Herman of Carinthia and Robert of Ketton. Al-Khwarizmī 's work transformed arithmetic by making the Indian /Arabic numerals and decimalisation familiar. His book on algebra , the al-Jabr, was translated by Robert of Chester in Segovia in 1145. Trigonometry became available. Fibonacci introduced quadratic equations. In fact, mathematics would not really advance until Descartes in the seventeenth century.

Other translators included Herman of Carinthia who translated largely for his learned patron, Thierry of Chartres; Dominic Gundisalvi (Domingo González) who was archdeacon of Segovia and worked in Toledo in the 1160s, especially on translating Avicenna; Robert of Ketton, archdeacon of Pamplona, an Englishman active in the 1140s and 1150s, who was an astronomer but made the first translation of the Qu'ran into Latin for the Abbot of Cluny; John of Seville, originally Jewish but baptised a Christian, was mainly translating astrology; Michael Scot (d1236) was from the north of England or Scotland and had studied throughout Europe before arriving in Toledo and learning Arabic. He translated at least two works by Aristotle, including *De animalibus* and his book on cosmography *De caelo et mundo*; as well as works by Averroës and Avicenna. He is also known to have worked in Rome, Bologna and Sicily and to have collaborated with Fibonacci. Both Scot and Fibonnaci were conduits between the translators in Toledo and Sicily.

Where else did Greek knowledge come back to Europe?

Southern Italy and Sicily were two other conduits of knowledge transfer. There had been a medical school in Salerno from the ninth century and for a time it was the most important in Europe. Its reputation was certainly high enough that the Bishop of Verdun went there for treatment in the 980s. It may have had its origins in the dispensary at the nearby monastery of Monte Cassino where manuscripts of Greek medicine, ie Galen, Hippocrates and Dioscorides, had been preserved. These could have come originally from the monastery set up by Cassiodorus at Squillace in Calabria.

More recent medical practice would have been known from Arabic practice in north Africa, and in 1077 an African called Constantine from Carthage arrived. There are few facts known about him except that he had travelled extensively and was self-taught. Shocked by the ignorance of the doctors in Salerno, he returned to Tunisia and acquired, over three years, a collection of up to date manuscripts of the latest Islamic medical practice. When he brought these back to Salerno, they were translated in to Latin, some by Constantine, and became standard medical texts in Europe for 500 years, even being printed in 1515 and 1536. Constantine converted to Christianity and became a monk at Monte Cassino where he died.

The Salerno school had a specialty in herbal cures and its situation on the coast near the port of Amalfi allowed import of herbs that were not found in Italy. It also developed practical experience in treating Crusaders returning from the taking of Jerusalem in 1099. The school's reputation helped medicine to become a recognised course of study in the universities that would open in the coming two centuries.

Sicily

Sicily has had a cosmopolitan mix of rulers throughout its history, in part as it was valued for its strategic position in the Mediterranean.

There were Greek colonies from ancient times. At the fall of the Roman empire it was taken over by the Ostrogoths. On being captured by the Byzantines, Greek was reintroduced as its language and Syracuse briefly became its capital. The Arabs invaded in 902 to be followed by the Normans. With such a history, the island had a very varied mix of Jews, Christians of differing varieties, as well as Muslims. Although the Norman conquest of 1091 was a very similar timing to the taking back of Toledo in 1085, there was a major difference in the translation programme for the Classics. In Sicily the translation into Latin was direct from the Greek rather than from Arabic. Scholarship was encouraged by King Roger II of Sicily and his son, William I, who were both Normans. Roger II created a kingdom which in its day was one of the most prosperous and powerful in Latin Christendom, which gave him the resources to create a cosmopolitan court and attract scholars from different traditions. The fact that Sicily was such a melting pot already would have been attractive to scholars from different backgrounds who would have brought their own copies of Greek texts too.

Some of the Greek documents came from the Byzantines often as part of trading relationships. One example is Ptolemy's *Almagest* which was brought to the court of King Roger II by Henry Aristippus, the archdeacon of Catania, and an envoy to Constantinople. This was translated into Latin in about 1160 by a scholar from the Salerno medical school, perhaps a few years before Gerard of Cremona's translation of it in Toledo.

The Normans also recreated Greek monasteries in their territories in southern Italy. Agents were sent to Greece to acquire books. One of the richest donations was to the monastery of St Salvador at Bordanaro near Messina. It was made by Scholarius who had been Roger's palace chaplain. This library included the *Mechanics of Hero*, Euclid's *Optics*, Aristotle, Anaxagoras, Themistius, Plutarch and the philosophers. Out of these, Aristippus translated Plato's *Meno* and *Phaedo* and the fourth book of Aristotle's *Meteorologica*. This was a substantial contribution to knowledge of the Greek classics as the only work of Plato known at the time was *Timaeus*, his thinking on science. Another translator was Eugenius of Palermo (1130–1202) who was an admiral and a poet, but known for translating Ptolemy's *Optics*.

Roger II ruled for 24 years until his death in 1154. He began a tradition of Norman, secular, academic courts that welcomed scholars of all backgrounds. His court hosted for 18 years one of the most important early geographers, **Al-Idrīsī** (1100–65), who was a Muslim scholar educated at Córdoba. He compiled the most advanced world map of its time, known as the *Tabula Rogeriana*, based on his knowledge of Islamic traders who had visited Africa, India and the Far East. This map divided the world into seven latitudinal sections, ten longitudinal sections, with maps for all seventy of these sections and detailed descriptions of the land and people on the territories shown. The map was in use for several hundred years and used by Columbus and Vasco da Gama.

After a not especially auspicious time, Roger II's grandson, Frederick took over the throne in 1208 becoming Frederick II. He was a scholar and founded the university in Naples. Two of the translators noted earlier, Fibonacci and Michael Scot were part of Frederick's entourage which moved around southern Italy so that they could be found in Palermo, Bologna, Pisa, Padua or Naples. Fibonnaci was able to discuss mathematics with Frederick who encouraged him to write a new book building on Euclid, the *Practica Geometriae*.

Frederick died in 1250 and the title King of Sicily soon passed to Charles of Anjou who continued the scholarly tradition which included translating Greek works directly into Latin, eg a number of Galen's works by Niccolò da Reggio.

By the time of Charles' death, the Normans had successfully established a home in Italy for itinerant scholars allowing cross fertilisation of ideas and learning in a secular atmosphere. Transmission of knowledge from the translation of Arabic and Greek had moved on to transformation into new knowledge much as had been seen on a larger scale in the House of Wisdom in Baghdad. Together with the work in Toledo, all this would lead to the Twelfth Century Renaissance, characterised by the re-introduction and absorption of Greek scientific and philosophical ideas. The Twelfth Century Renaissance will be looked at in the next chapter; the Italian Renaissance which would begin 100 years later and gradually see the restoration to western Europe of the Greek literary canon, is the subject of Chapter 6.

The preparation of the pulp and papermaking in the Islamic world.

Eadwine the Scribe, c1147.

V

THE TWELFTH CENTURY RENAISSANCE

Logic has made me hated in this world. **Peter Abelard**

As Chapter 3 pointed out, the Carolingian Renaissance of the ninth century had helped to halt the decline in the knowledge of the Latin classics and Latin language which had occurred in the "Dark Ages". It was a period of conservation rather than innovation. It saved many of the Roman literary classics by encouraging copying of them in the monasteries and, in doing so, gave us the Caroline minuscule handwriting. And the creation of many more educational establishments did lay a foundation for further advances.

However, its geographical extent was limited to the Frankish empire which meant principally France, a greater Germany that took in Austria, Switzerland, and Czechoslovakia, together with the Benelux countries and northern Italy. It was a movement dependent on the court and Palace of Charlemagne. When the Carolingian dynasty ended in 882, the good work dissipated, and Europe fractured again in to a land of barbarian invasions, war lords, and general anarchy.

Europe by the twelfth century was settling down again. There was greater agricultural productivity which meant more food; political boundaries were more stable; there was a common religion; commerce and trade had increased along with demand for improved infrastructure and regulation; economies worked with money and contracts rather than barter. Windmills, paper, magnetic compasses and the astrolabe were technological innovations. The new wealth and resulting population increase had led to urbanisation, which in turn brought the need for civil administrators and lawyers, which in turn meant a need for greater literacy and numeracy. By this time, the monasteries were in decline and their role in providing education had moved to the cathedrals which were situated in the new urban settings.

Life was far from ideal for many. On the negative side there was warfare in the form of the Crusades; persecution of Jews in France and Germany; Christian infighting such as the suppression of the Cathars in France; and the Reconquista in Spain. However, as the incursions of Vikings ended, life became more settled with the Norman feudal system in France, England and Italy.

How easy was it to absorb all of the new ideas?

At this time, theology was central to all intellectual endeavour. Christian thinkers were keen to understand the nature of the divine, and to see how the ordered and rational nature of the universe gave proof of its creator. This meant reconciling the Book of Genesis with the new ideas of Greek and Islamic science. The intention was to create a coherent philosophy of nature which could exist in harmony with Christian revelation. The principal minds brought to bear on this were Robert Grosseteste (1168-1253) who was Chancellor of Oxford University and later Bishop of Lincoln; Roger Bacon (c1219-c1292); Albertus Magnus (c1200-1280); and his pupil, Thomas Aquinas (1225-1274).

The work of Plato with its central doctrine of design in the universe was acceptable as it could be seen in a religious light. It was certainly preferable to the animistic beliefs in a variety of gods and spirits who controlled the seas, rivers, and mountains. Aristotle, whose work was largely available by 1200 and all translated by 1260, was much harder to absorb within Christian teaching. For this reason there was a reliance on commentators on his work to make it more palatable. Both of the main commentators were Islamic: Avicenna was mainly used until 1230, after which Averroës was preferred.

Aristotle was more precise and analytical than Plato. The controversial elements in Aristotle were that the universe was eternal and that the soul was part of the body and died with it. His philosophical system claimed that the world was intelligible without revelation and could be explained by using reason: observation, measurement, logical inference, demonstrable cause and effect. That the universe operates through natural cause and effect then left no room for the omnipotence of God, miracles or human free will. This was in conflict with Biblical truth whereby God knows when the sparrow falls and the numbers of hairs on our head. Traditionalists were fearful that philosophy and theology could end up opposed, leaving a conflict between Athens and Jerusalem.

Between 1210 and 1240, Aristotle's natural philosophy was banned at the university of Paris by the conservative governing body to avoid contamination of its accepted theological instruction. The idea was to produce an expurgated version so that students could still study the useful and non controversial parts of Aristotle's writing. No such document has been passed down to us and by 1255 all of Aristotle was deemed acceptable.

Much of the credit for finding a way through the perceived incompatibilities is down to Thomas Aquinas who devised a "Christian Aristotelianism" that reconciled the differences by various ingenious arguments.

What was the role of the universities?

After the Carolingian Renaissance, higher education was vested in the cathedral schools which had taken over teaching from the monasteries. The most important of these were in northern France, eg Chartres, Laon, Rheims, Paris and Orleans. The purpose of teaching in these institutions was production of educated cathedral clergy, although lay people were accepted. Students would travel from one to another in search of a suitable master and there were no hindrances of fixed curricula and periods of study.

The traditional curriculum of the religious schools had involved the basic trivium (grammar, logic and rhetoric) which then passed to the more scientific quadrivium (arithmetic, geometry, music and astronomy). This system had been the basis of higher education since Hellenistic Greece and Rome.

The growth in new knowledge and rediscovery of Classical knowledge entering Europe in the twelfth century led to an attempt to squeeze the increased logic, mathematics, and astronomy into this system; but it still left out law, theology and medicine. Although we have seen centres of higher education in Greece, Gondishapur, Alexandria and Baghdad in earlier times, the university as a learned corporation with faculties, curricula and academic degrees began in the twelfth century.

Universitas meant in Roman law a sworn society of individuals. The early European universities were effectively guilds of masters (the professors), journeymen (graduates) and apprentices (students) whose aim was vocational education to produce priests, doctors or lawyers. They had no campuses or buildings but were located in cities where rooms could be hired for teaching and students could find lodging. Eventually, the college system gave greater protection for students and better control of behaviour for the masters.

The University in Paris was the only one to grow directly from a cathedral school, in this case Notre Dame. The Chancellor of the cathedral licensed the teachers. The most famous teacher was Abelard (1079-1142), but tutors came from across Europe including Thierry of Chartres, William of Conches, John of Salisbury and Peter Lombard. Other early universities were found at Bologna (1088), Salamanca (1134), Oxford (1167) with many more, such as Cambridge (1209), Montpellier (1220), and Padua (1222), starting shortly after 1200.

In these universities the seven liberal arts of the trivium and quadrivium continued to be taught. Grammar was based on Priscian and Donatus; logic had been greatly expanded with the rediscovery of Aristotle; arithmetic and music still depended on Boethius; geometry was now based on Euclid; astronomy on Ptolemy; and medicine on Galen and Hippocrates.

It will be worth exploring how the other subjects had changed with the revival of the Greek classics:

Science

The Twelfth Century Renaissance is marked by the change in thinking about science, even though it was still regarded as part of philosophy, ie natural philosophy. Until 1100, the *Etymologies* of Isidore of Seville was regarded as the sum of human knowledge. This had to a large extent superseded the *Natural History* of Pliny the Elder (AD23-79) which was still read as was Boethius. Euclid's *Elements* in Latin was only known by fragments of Books 1-4, and those without proofs or diagrams. Similarly unknown in Latin were the Galenic corpus and Ptolemy's *Almagest*.

Isidore of Seville (c.560-636) is regarded as the last scholar of the ancient world. He was Bishop of Seville for thirty years and amassed a large library of Christian and Classical writing in both Latin and Greek. His library was arranged in 14 armaria (book cases); 7 were devoted to theology; 2 to poetry; and one each for history, moral theology, law, medicine, and one for miscellaneous. The library probably contained some 450 books, a sizeable collection at the time. He used this library to write the *Etymologies* which was effectively an encyclopaedia of all knowledge known to mankind at that time, including science. One of its shortcomings was the lack of Greek knowledge. Isidore knew no Greek. The Romans, being bilingual, had not translated writers like Galen, Hippocrates and Euclid. That meant that Isidore could only pass on whatever knowledge from ancient Greece had appeared in compilations and summaries from Roman and later writers. However, like the work of Boethius, this compilation was one of the most common books found in medieval libraries throughout Europe and preserved some classical fragments now lost.

Astronomy was transformed by Adelard of Bath's translation; al-Khwarizmī 's astronomical tables; and the translations of Ptolemy's *Almagest* in both Toledo and Sicily. Aristotle's *Physics* and *Meteorology* came from the Arabic versions to which can be added Ibn al-Haytham's *Optics*. Medicine benefited from the full versions of Galen and Hippocrates together with the Muslim commentaries and additions. Avicenna's *Canon* was accepted in Europe only slightly later in the thirteenth century. Despite the improvement on what had gone before, Greco-Arabic medicine was still at the stage of the four humours (blood, phlegm, black bile and yellow bile), blood-letting with leeches, etc. But to scholastics of the time it meant that these theoretical schemas raised medicine a cut above the "illiterate barbers, fortune tellers, alchemists, old women, converted Jews and Saracens" with whom they competed.

Despite the plentiful examples of scientific observation and experiment from the Greeks and Arabs that were now known, the Christians of the twelfth century and Middle Ages were loathe to follow their example. Twelfth century science showed a reverence for the written word and meant learning rather than discovery. Astronomy was what Ptolemy had reasoned it to be; natural history was what Pliny had observed; medicine was what Galen had described; geography was limited to the study of books, not even maps let alone travel; physics the logical interpretation of Aristotle. The scholastic study of the new works showed an acceptance and respect for the authority of these books, but little willingness for testing them, experimentation, verification and proof. These would have to wait for another three centuries.

Law

The Romans were never particularly philosophical, but they were good at law. The *Corpus Juris Civilis* of the Emperor Justinian, came from the eastern Roman Empire in the sixth century. It comprised the *Code* of imperial legislation; the *Digest*, or summary of the Roman jurists; the *Institutes* or textbook for the law schools; and the *Novels* or later additions to the law. Of these, the *Digest* was the most important as it preserved the written reasoning for juristic analysis and technique. But it had fallen out of usage from 603-1076 with the demise of Roman administration and only extracts and summaries were known.

After the collapse of the Roman Empire, Europe's laws were made locally and relied on tradition and custom which was often not written down. The twelfth century saw the recovery of the full corpus of Roman law. The recovery is attributed to Irnerius (c1050-c1125), a lawyer in Bologna who wrote glosses and separated law from rhetoric in teaching which eventually led to the University at Bologna becoming the pre-eminent university for legal studies. This was encouraged by the economic development and political consolidation in Italy at the time which required a better legal basis than local custom. Roman law spread from here to France, Spain, Germany and even Scotland.

Bologna was also important for canon law which was the law of the Roman Catholic church. In the twelfth century, canon law was important for ordinary citizens as well as the clergy. It governed not just church property and conduct by church officials, but such everyday matters as marriage, wills, and sexual conduct right up to heresy with punishments from imprisonment to death. A monk called Gratian living in Bologna around 1140 produced a summary of all the relevant canon law into a directory called the *Decretum*. The highest authority was the Pope and the various Church councils. Although it had links to Roman law by virtue of the Catholic Church, canon law was applicable in countries such as England that had never accepted Roman law. English common law was an oddity in that it was not taught in universities in the twelfth century but was learnt in the Inns of Court in London.

Many students at Paris who began a course in Theology would transfer after two years to Law as they could see a more lucrative future.

Language and literature

The Twelfth Century Renaissance was more about philosophy and science than literature. The prejudice against enjoying pagan poetry and drama in a very Christian time remained a dilemma that had long existed. That said, the cathedral schools of Chartres and Orleans retained an active appreciation of the Classics. Most of the Roman classical writers were largely known again by this time. Roman writers who were popular included Virgil, Horace, Ovid, Lucan, Juvenal, Persius, Cicero, Seneca, Sallust and Terence. Beginning to circulate were Quintilian, Livy and the first eight plays of Plautus. Rare copies of Catullus, Tibullus, Propertius, Tacitus and Lucretian were little known or still undiscovered. The Twelfth Century Renaissance did lead to many more copies of these being made than had survived from the Carolingian Renaissance, and some texts such as the *Natural Questions* of Seneca, are only known from the twelfth century as the earlier Carolingian copies perished. But one of the problems was always that the more a text is copied, then the more errors that creep in.

The emphasis on the works of Aristotle, logic, metaphysics, natural science, medicine and law, squeezed out the previous interest in the Roman literary classics. Study of the these Roman classics was not even included in the curriculum at Paris. It was only in the fourteenth century that Petrarch and Boccaccio re-awakened the appreciation of the Greek and Roman literary classics. Their writing heralded the more famous Italian Renaissance which will be looked at in the next chapter.

Philosophy

Twelfth century thinkers were predisposed towards the work of Aristotle because he had been summarised by Boethius whose writings were still influential. Muslim writers such as Avicenna and Averroës had written extensive commentaries on Aristotle's works which had been translated into Latin and this added to his appeal. Plato was little known at this time, only the first fifty three chapters of his dialogue *Timaeus* on the natural world being available. Another appeal to an age that loved manuals and textbooks was the concise and systematic style of Aristotle.

The whole corpus of Aristotle was not translated until about 1260, the thirteenth century additions being *Metaphysics, On Animals, Ethics, Politics, Rhetoric and Poetics.*

Scholasticism

Teaching in Paris and several of the other new universities followed a rigid pattern. A tutor would give a lecture in which he set out a thesis. This would be followed by arguments for and against, ie the antithesis, and these would draw on citations from various authorities on the subject. The tutor would then help students draw a conclusion. Sources cited were mainly the Bible and the Church Fathers but Classical writers could also be used.

Peter Abelard (1079-1142) was particularly associated with this approach and wrote a book entitled *Sic et non* which appeared in the 1130s. This listed 158 questions on dogma and gave many conflicting sources to form antitheses. Whilst giving guidance as to how to reach a conclusion, he refrained from giving one for each question. The Church took exception as it felt the task of the tutor was to give direction; that meant the role of the Church was to make clear its accepted hierarchical judgements.

Slightly later, the Bishop of Paris, **Peter Lombard** (1096–1160), wrote a similar book entitled *The Four Books of Sentences*. In the pro and con arguments, hundreds of sources were cited. However, Lombard gave the right answers in conformity with the thinking of the Church and only three of all the sources cited were not from Christian writing.

To show the impact of the re-introduction of Classical thinking, **Thomas Aquinas** produced the *Summa Theologica* between 1265 and 1274. It contained an estimated 2.2 million words. Like Abelard, he produced questions with sources giving arguments for and against; in Aquinas' case, there were 631 such questions. However, by now the Greek classics had been absorbed and 3,500 of the citations came from Aristotle alone. The achievement of Aquinas was in assimilating Aristotle into a theologically acceptable system of thought, as Avicenna and Averroës had done for Islam two hundred years before. Averroës had by this time become known as "The Commentator" on Aristotle and Aquinas cites him 503 times in the *Summa*. This dialectical form of teaching continued for a few hundred years but was gradually undermined by the growth of humanism and Protestantism.

One of the advantages of Scholasticism was that the new universities had a striking uniformity across Europe. The curriculum based on a modified trivium, meaning less grammar and more logic, was common to all. The uniformity, together with Latin as the common language of education, did allow professors to teach at different universities and gain experience from their travels. Students were also able to move around Europe seeking out the teachers they would most benefit from so that there was a surprising amount of mobility in the twelfth century educational world. And there were specialisms such as law at Bologna, medicine at Montpellier, and theology at Paris.

However, looking back at ancient Greece, institutions such as the Academy and the Lyceum had been known for having rival philosophies. Scholasticism, in trying to unify all knowledge in a system of logic, lacked flexibility and any room to adapt, innovate and introduce originality. It was looking tired so that the challenge from humanism in the fourteenth century gradually led to its being superseded. Humanism, which will be looked at in the next chapter, was less dogmatic and formulaic and so allowed greater scope and elasticity for teaching.

The Ten Storytellers, from a 1492 Italian edition of *The Decameron*.

Leonardo Bruni, from a manuscript in the Biblioteca Medicea Laurenziana.

VI

HUMANISM AND
THE ITALIAN RENAISSANCE

Humanists conceived the revival of antiquity as creative obeisance; retrieving ancient learning was not an inferior chore but a proof of their own high talents. This was a just appraisal, for until printing became widespread the rescue of lost texts from oblivion was the main path to scholarly progress.
David Lowenthal, The Past is a Foreign Country, 1985

The Latin texts of the major Roman writers had been known and used throughout the Medieval period. But their use was mainly as sources of information, fine phrases, and anecdotes. They were working tools rather than being admired for their literary merit or as works of art. The emphasis on science, medicine, mathematics and philosophy in the Twelfth Century Renaissance was to some extent at the expense of reviving Roman classical literature.

Whereas Roman writing had been known if not appreciated in western Europe in medieval times, Greek classical literature in terms of plays, poems, and collected oratory was largely unknown. This was because the ability to read Greek was almost non-existent. Greek science, philosophy, mathematics and medicine had been reintroduced thanks to the Arabic translations. But the Arabs had not been interested in Greek literature.

In this later Renaissance, the Italian humanists and their later counterparts in northern Europe, tried to rediscover and collect these ancient literary texts. They also wanted to try to reinhabit the world of the Classical writers, so that learning Greek and improving their Latin was an essential part of trying to emulate their heroes when it came to their own writing.

The period covered is from the late thirteenth century to the mid sixteenth century. By the end of that period, most of what could be recovered from Classical antiquity was available in print, either in the original language or in translation of some form, so that Greek classical literature was known as well as Roman.

The seeds of the Italian Renaissance, the cultural movement known as humanism, can be traced back as early as the late thirteenth century when **Lovato Lovati** (1241-1309), a judge in Padua, and his small circle were finding manuscripts of Roman poetry in the monastery of Pomposa, in the Po delta, and the cathedral library of Verona. Their aim was to reconnect with the Classical texts, to understand them, and to imitate them with their own poetry or elegant Latin prose: *translatio, imitatio* and preferably *aemulatio*.

Why did the fifteenth century Renaissance start in Italy?

The social and economic context for the fifteenth century Renaissance was not dissimilar from that of the twelfth century. The Black Death of the mid 1300s led to the loss of some one third of Europe's population. Those that survived became more prosperous as wage rates rose because of labour scarcity, and many others benefited from earlier inheritance. The feudal system had broken down and there was more social mobility. Italy was developing commerce and trade through better banking, a working legal system, and improved accounting. It was also characterised by urban centres with a professional class that had the training and wherewithal to take up Classical interests and to put into practice some of the civic example from antiquity. Whereas most of Europe was still predominantly agrarian with wealth locked up in the land and the castles of its owners, the new merchants and professionals based in the cities of Italy had the disposable and mobile wealth rather than the nobility.

There was after the Black Death a general dissatisfaction with life and pessimism about the future. God had been seen to fail humanity and the message from the Church that mankind was sinful, wretched, helpless and fallen, was not one that people wanted to hear. There was a searching for hope and optimism, for freedom and self-determination, a new creative channel. What was needed was a "rebirth". Intellectuals wanted an end to the decline of the arts and humanities during what Flavio Biondo termed the "Middle Ages", which had stretched from antiquity to their own time.

It would mean individuals finding the self-confidence to carve out a new future by their own efforts. Ironically, the blueprint that they began to search for was 1,500 years old. However, by emulating the exemplary works of the Greek and Roman writers, artists and thinkers, even striving to surpass them, contemporary artists and writers might restore the arts and letters to their former grandeur. Living in city states with visual reminders of Roman greatness all around them helped many in this feeling that studying Rome's past might lead to a renewal of a more civilised way of life. Foremost in this thinking were the humanists.

In Renaissance Italy, this desire to know and to match the excellence of the ancients often engendered passionate endeavour. Humanism was very much a literary movement and also consciously secular in terms of wanting to read literature that went beyond the narrow prescription of the Catholic Church. The growth in printing from the 1460s allowed circulation of affordable books that would help reduce the dependence on ecclesiastical sources for learning, even though many of the early printed books were of a religious nature.

Universities were not the principal channel of the movement. The main strengths of Italy's universities were law and medicine, which were essentially secular, and a great many of the humanists had trained as lawyers. There is a theory that the resurgence of Roman law at universities like Bologna had encouraged lawyers to reconnect with antiquity. Certainly the Italian academic focus on law had attracted the brightest and best to follow that profession in either civil or canon law. The law was also taught in non-university cities, eg Florence, and so Italian learning had more of a focus on practical problems of government and administration than the metaphysical and theological training north of the Alps. Grammar and rhetoric were linked to the teaching of law which encouraged a focus on the *Code* and *Digest* rather than the Bible.

The Italian humanists revised the university trivium to exclude logic and include history, moral philosophy (ethics) and especially poetry instead. This became known as the *Studia Humanitatis*, from which the term humanist comes. It spread throughout Europe and was deemed the appropriate educational foundation for future civil servants, clergy and the learned professions. The ideal of a liberal education grounded in the Classical languages and literature survived for hundreds of years in universities such as Oxford and Cambridge.

Why was Florence the centre of the Italian Renaissance?

Florence of the mid to late fourteenth century differed from other Italian cities such as Genoa, Venice and Tuscan republics such as Pisa and Siena by its wealth and industry. Textiles, especially wool, were the main industry and the banking firms were international in their dealings. The city also avoided being run by a single powerful family, so that its citizens kept a keen interest in maintaining a flexible local government under their control.

Many of the most famous figures of the Italian Renaissance are linked to Florence:

Petrarch (Francesco Petrarca)

Petrarch (1304-74) is one of the great early figures of the humanist movement. He united the literary and scholarly aspects of humanism and tried to revive the ideals of ancient Rome within a Christian framework. Born in Tuscany, his father was a Florentine lawyer. His father was attached to the papal curia then based in Avignon, so that Petrarch grew up in that city. Like many humanists, Petrarch also trained as a lawyer but he rejected this as a career path. He had also experienced the scholasticism of the French education system and rejected that too. He felt Aristotle and the Church Fathers were deified and had become the subject of servile adherence; whilst dialectic was made an end in itself.

Petrarch loved the poetry of Virgil and Ovid, the moral thought of Seneca and Cicero, and the histories of Tacitus and Livy. He saw in these writers a virtue to be aspired to that embraced all the best qualities of excellence in mankind. Their work contrasted with the Latin of the schools, monasteries and administration which had become practical but clumsy and inelegant.

A great poet in his own right, he was crowned in Rome as the second poet laureate since antiquity in 1341 at the age of thirty six. While based in Avignon he indulged his love of Classical poetry by visiting libraries in monasteries and cathedrals in search of Roman classical manuscripts. Petrarch is also thought to have been the first to use the term "Dark Ages" to describe the period when the Classics were unknown after the fall of the Roman Empire.

Boccaccio

Giovanni Boccaccio (1313-75) was the son of a Florentine merchant and grew up in the city. Best known for the *Decameron*, Boccaccio also later wrote *Genealogia deorum gentilium* which is an encyclopaedic work on the Greek and Roman myths and gods. The later work was written after he became a humanist through his friendship with Petrarch, whom he regarded as his teacher. *The Decameron*, is a series of novellas telling of a group of friends sheltering in a villa outside Florence from the Black Death of 1348. Boccaccio lived for many years in Naples but is seen as a loyal Florentine and did much to link Petrarch's legacy to the city.

Coluccio Salutati

Salutati (1331–75) trained as a lawyer in Bologna and only moved to Florence in 1374. He became devoted to the city and repaid his adoption of it with being a brilliant civil servant . In his spare time he was devoted to the Classics and built a large library of 800 books. He used his legal mind to edit many of these manuscripts, delighting in correcting punctuation and spelling made by scribes. In his capacity of Chancellor of Florence, he was instrumental in bringing Manuel Chrysoloras (see below) to the city. This invitation marked the revival of Greek studies in Europe. He also encouraged many younger humanist scholars, including his successor as Chancellor, Leonardo Bruni.

Salutati's tragic family life may also have given him the motivation to engage in higher pursuits: plague had killed his father, four of his brothers and sisters, both of his wives, and two of his sons.

Leonardo Bruni

Leonardo Bruni (1369–1444) moved to Florence to study law but was greatly influenced by the teaching of Manuel Chrysoloras. He gave up law and dedicated himself to studying the Classics under the patronage of Salutati. After ten years attached to the papacy, he returned to Florence as Chancellor. In his spare time he produced new translations of works by Plato, Aristotle, Demosthenes and Plutarch. He managed to write biographies of Petrarch and Boccaccio as well as a history of Florence.

Perhaps his greatest contribution was to find in the works of Aristotle a way around the biggest dilemma facing many Italians of his time. The Bible and adherents such as St Francis had preached poverty and abnegation. Many of the rich had assuaged their guilt by giving money and land to the monasteries and churches to pay their way to heaven. Bruni could see from his Classical reading that the possession of external goods affords an opportunity for the exercise of virtue. He found in Martial the observation that poverty could restrict a man's virtues. From this stems a justification of wealth which after caring for family and house, means using it for good causes. That may mean anything from patronage of the arts to ecclesiastical decoration, but doing it without the feeling of guilt that had gone with Christian teaching.

Poggio Bracciolini

Bracciolini (1380-1459) also eventually became Chancellor of Florence. He studied law in Florence where his talents became apparent and he was befriended by Salutati and Niccolò de' Niccoli, who was another humanist and a famous book collector of Classical texts.

Most of his long career was spent in the service of seven Popes where his excellent Latin and beautiful writing, a form of Caroline minuscule which was used as the model for the roman typeface, were much admired. (Niccolò de' Niccoli developed a cursive script that would later be known as italic in printed form). Despite his service in the Curia, he remained a layman. Poggio's fame is in his relentless tracking down of Classical manuscripts in monasteries. As noted in Chapter 3, it was during the Council of Constance, 1414-18, when he began his famous searches of Swiss and German monastic libraries searching for Classical texts. Among the monasteries visited were St Gall, Reichenau, and Fulda. He later searched the libraries of French monasteries such as Cluny, where he found speeches of Cicero, and Monte Cassino and Bobbio nearer home.

The list of texts discovered is too long to note, but the most famous were copies of Vitruvius' *De Architectura* and the *De Rerum Natura* by Lucretius. The Vitruvius owes its survival to the recopying of work in the Carolingian Renaissance and the copy found by Poggio in 1414 had survived at the monastery library of St Gall. It was used as the inspiration for **Andrea Palladio** in the sixteenth century who transformed architecture by using classical Greek and Roman style. Palladio had been born Andrea di Pietro della Gondola, but one of his patrons renamed him Palladio after the Greek goddess of wisdom, Pallas Athene, known to us as Athena. His work, and the book he wrote clarifying the principles of Vitruvius and giving the practical means of employing them, influenced architects throughout Europe including Inigo Jones in England. It allowed the building of villas for the rich, new elite who were wanting country residences in emulation of Cicero and Virgil.

At Fulda was discovered the work *De Rerum Natura* in Latin by Lucretius (99–55BC) which reveals the world view of the Greek philosopher Epicurus. The writing of Lucretius was quite unlike any other Latin text. In part this is because it could be deemed scientific, but mainly as it was quite revolutionary and forward looking. He wrote that the natural world was nothing to do with divine intervention but was made of atoms that evolve and reproduce. He did not believe in an afterlife and felt all organised religion was superstitious. Contrary to the prevailing Christian view that pain and suffering in this world would bring joy in the next, Lucretius espoused that the highest human goal was the enhancement of pleasure and reduction of pain. *De Rerum Natura* is an extraordinary book that became the subject of Stephen Greenblatt's 2011 Pulitzer prize winning book about Poggio's discovery titled *The Swerve: how the world became modern*. (Without wishing to lessen Poggio's achievements, it should be noted that Lovato Lovati (1241-1309) was familiar with Lucretius some 150 years earlier).

Bracciolini wrote many books in beautiful Latin, including a continuation of the history of Florence begun by Bruni, but in the style of Livy and Sallust.

Fine Arts

Florence was also blessed with some of the greatest artistic talents of the Renaissance. The originality of **Masaccio**(1401-28) in being the first painter since Classical times to use mathematically correct lines of perspective; the dome on Florence's cathedral and many other local architectural works by **Brunelleschi** (1377-1446) who had taught Masaccio the secrets of one-point perspective; the Baptistry doors in Florence by **Ghiberti** (1378-1455) after he won the 1401 competition; and sculptures such as *David* and *St. George* by **Donatello** (1386-1466). These early triumphs set the standard for later artists and helped make Florence the leading city of the Renaissance movement. In an earlier age, it had also been the birthplace of **Dante Alighieri** (1265-1321) who wrote *The Divine Comedy* during his many years in exile from the city.

The brief Florentine Golden Age would build on these roots under the patronage of Lorenzo de Medici (1449-92), attracting poets and philosophers like Pico della Mirandola and Marsilio Ficino, and brief acquaintances with the artists Michelangelo and Leonardo da Vinci. The *Oration on the Dignity of Man* by Pico della Mirandola (1463-94) is often seen as the manifesto of the Renaissance. The Golden Age ended on the death of Lorenzo and the rise of the puritanical Girolamo Savonarola (1452-98).

At a later stage, the Italian Renaissance developed what the musical world understands as opera. Around 1600, Florentine humanists tried to revive the Greek drama with the original chorus becoming singing parts. The earliest such opera known today is Monteverdi's *L'Orfeo* composed in 1607.

Recovery of Greek literary texts

The south of Italy had retained a small Greek speaking population but few were bilingual. Links with the northern Renaissance cities were geographically poor and as a result they played no part in the revival of Greek learning. It was the trading and diplomatic links with Constantinople that saw the growth in links with Greek speakers as the Byzantine empire came to an end before the final Ottoman Turkish takeover in 1453. A Byzantine diplomat, Manuel Chrysoloras was the man who unlocked for the Italians the hidden treasures of Greek classical literature.

Manuel Chrysoloras (c1350–1415) was Greek, a courtier in Constantinople and friend of the Byzantine Emperor. He was selected for a diplomatic mission to Europe to mobilise support in overcoming the threat from the Ottoman Turks.

In 1390/1 Chrysoloras was in Venice at a time when the early Renaissance scholars were aware of the Greek classics, but were unable to read the few Greek manuscripts then available. Arabic translations had mainly been of scientific and medical works and not the literary canon.

The chancellor of Florence, Colucio Salutati, offered Chrysoloras a professorship at the Academy of Florence requesting him to obtain a long list of Greek classical works which would be the foundation of a library for Italian students. Chrysoloras spent three years in Florence from 1397 teaching Greek and helping translate some of the books into Latin. He wrote a Greek grammar *Erotemate* (Questions) which would be printed in 1484. His pupils would be the first Italians to master classical Greek for 700 years: Guarino da Verona went on to be a Professor of Greek at Ferrara; Leonardo Bruni would translate many of the Greek classics and eventually succeed Salutati as Chancellor of Florence.

Well before the fall of Constantinople to the Ottomans in 1453, Greeks had brought some 1,000 Classical manuscripts to Italy. More refugees from Constantinople appeared after 1453 and they were keen to teach Greek and copy manuscripts. As the revival of Roman classics spread an interest in the Greek writers mentioned in them, so the demand for learning Greek increased. Venice was the centre for Greek speaking refugees. One of the most important figures of this time was **Bessarion of Trebizond** (c1400–72) who had been educated in Constantinople. He was sent to Ferrara by the Orthodox Church in 1438 as part of a delegation to a council convened by Pope Eugenius IV to try to heal the rift with the Roman Catholic church. Impressing the Pope, he was made a cardinal, which was very unusual for an Orthodox cleric. On two occasions, in 1455 and 1471, he was nearly elected pope.

Cardinal Bessarion stayed on in Rome and his home became a centre for humanists. The attraction was his large library of Greek manuscripts and his generous hospitality and encouragement to any scholar pursuing Greek studies. He also travelled in Europe cultivating scholars and collecting books. Perhaps the most famous scholar was Johann Müller, who is better known as Regiomontanus (1436–76), encountered on a journey to Vienna. Müller was commissioned by Bessarion to produce a more concise version of Ptolemy's *Almagest*. This duly appeared in 1462 and was half the length of the original, contained updates from Arabic astronomers, and was better structured and clearer to users. It was called *The Epitome* and was printed in 1496, enabling astronomers such as Kepler, Copernicus and Galileo to improve on Ptolemy's researches dating back 1400 years.

Bessarion shared his interests in the equally scholarly Pope Nicholas V. They were both interested in mathematics and Pope Nicholas was keen to enlarge the Vatican library. They sponsored translations of Greek mathematicians such as Archimedes, and the lesser known Proclus, Hero, Apollonius and Diophantus. Renaissance architecture relied on mathematics and Brunelleschi could not have constructed the dome on the cathedral in Florence without applied geometry.

As a scholar and a translator from Greek into Latin, Bessarion contributed to the Renaissance rediscovery of classical Greek and Roman culture. He formed an important library of Greek classics. His library of 745 manuscripts (482 Greek) was eventually bequeathed to Venice as a public library as that was where most Greek speakers lived, and by this time printing had begun in Italy with Venice as the most important centre. He signed an agreement with the Doge in 1468 which committed Venice to construct a building and for the books to be made available to all scholars. When he died his collection was housed in Rome and Urbino and the books were transported to the Doge's palace. There they were stored until 1531. It took until 1588 for the Biblioteca Marciana to be constructed, a building designed by Sansovino opposite the Doge's palace.

It would still take a considerable time before Greek studies could reach the refinement and support of Latin studies in most of Europe. Hay (1977) suggests it was not until the eighteenth century that they reached the fifteenth century level of Latin studies.

Fibonnaci was encountered in Chapter 4 as having made Hindu/ Arabic numerals widely used in Europe in the twelfth century. Some of his more complex mathematical ideas had not been taken up. It was another Italian, **Luca Pacioli** ((1447-1517) who traced them to a copy of the *Liber abbaci* in a Venetian library. Pacioli's *Summa de Arithmetica* gave the world double-entry bookkeeping as well as bringing together summaries of earlier writers on algebra and geometry. This book in printed form helped to transmit many Classical and Arabic mathematical ideas, especially as it was written in Italian. Pacioli became a Franciscan friar and went on to write *De Divina Proportione*, which proposed that mathematics such as the Golden ratio was so pure it must have divine origin. He became a close friend of Leonardo da Vinci and the two collaborated on both mathematical and sacred matters.

What of the Renaissance outside Italy?

The Italian humanists had taken the lead in recovering Greek and Roman classics and their artists had brought a naturalism not seen in the earlier Middle Ages. The appreciation of classical Latin had shown the benefits of a literary language with fixed spelling, set grammatical rules and yet rich in expression. This would, by example, improve the consistency of vernacular languages and printing would shortly go on to further help codify them. In England, France, Germany and Spain there was no accepted national language, and the variety of local dialects was making communication difficult.

The prominence of legal training in the Italian humanists would also influence countries to the north giving a viable alternative to the previous emphasis on theology. Italian commerce and government was, by and large, ahead of the rest of Europe. Northern Europe had strong monarchy and a rural nobility in contrast to the regionalism and bourgeois values of Italy.

The Italian Renaissance had shown three stages: the early period to about 1370 with isolated geniuses such as Petrarch; the succeeding Florentine century which led the way in art and ideas; and the period from 1450-1550 when the princely courts and the papal court in Rome took over as rich patrons. It was only at the third stage when northern Europe could engage with the changes being brought about because of the familiarity with a princely and aristocratic society. Even then, it took until the early 1500s before scholars and painters were part of the courtly entourage north of the Alps.

How were the new ideas of the Renaissance transmitted?

The transmission of new ideas to the north came through Italian humanists travelling north; northern European scholars and diplomats travelling to Italy; and the increased circulation of books that came with printing.

I can give examples of all three from my own experience of working at Wells Cathedral. **Polydore Vergil** (1470-1555) was an Italian humanist, scholar and priest sent to England in 1502 by the Pope to be a deputy collector of church taxes. He was much celebrated at court and could count English humanists such as Thomas More, Cuthbert Tunstall, Thomas Linacre and John Colet as friends. Polydore was made Archdeacon of Wells although most of his fourteen years in the post was spent in London. He wrote a number of books but his *Anglica Historia*, a history of England commissioned by Henry VII, is in a style that completely overshadowed the previous authorities such as Geoffrey of Monmouth and Gildas. It is his best known book in England.

Going the other way to Italy is shown by **John Gunthorpe** (d. 1498) who was Dean of Wells from 1472 until his death. Gunthorpe was an early English humanist who studied the classics at Ferrara under Guarino da Verona before joining the papal court in Rome. Guarino had himself been a pupil of Manuel Chrysoloras. Gunthorpe's excellent Latin made him a diplomat in the court of Edward IV and he went on diplomatic missions to Castile. His library reflected the curriculum of the *Studia Humanitatis.*

And one of the Latin books gifted by Gunthorpe to the library at Wells Cathedral is the beautiful *Historia Naturalis* by Pliny the Elder in the 1472 edition printed in Venice by Nicholas Jenson. Jenson's role in early printing will be described in the next chapter.

How did the ideas of the Italian Renaissance influence Britain?

When the great Dutch humanist **Desiderius Erasmus** (1466–1536) visited England in 1499 he was very complimentary about the scholarship of the group of humanists noted above with whom Polydore Vergil had already connected. Many of these were in holy orders in contrast to the leaders of the movement in Italy who were laymen and often lawyers.

However by 1500 there was already in England a move to increase the number of laymen in civil administration. This was mainly as many more were required, but also as hiring and firing Roman Catholic priests (the only alternative) could be problematic with their various forms of immunity under canon law. The impact of the Renaissance in northern Europe is complex because by the early 1500s it is co-existing with the Protestant Reformation, and this is a factor that did not apply in Italy or Spain.

The lay clerks were required to improve their Latin as a result of the elegant neo-classical examples being set in Italy and beyond. Perhaps the main thrust of the English response to the Renaissance is the foundation of new colleges at Oxford and Cambridge as well as the foundation of grammar schools. It was men in holy orders who founded many of these: the Bishop of Rochester at St John's Cambridge; the bishop of Winchester at Corpus Christi, Oxford.

The most important long term institution was the refounding in 1509 of St Paul's school in London by the leading humanist, John Colet, who was the Dean of St Paul's cathedral. He decreed that the school should be secular and ensured that the first High Master, John Lily, was not in holy orders. Despite the name and location, the school was founded by the Mercers' Company, a trade body, and so was independent of church control. With 153 pupils, it was double the size of Eton or Winchester.

The statutes of St Paul's School became the template for the large growth in new grammar schools that soon followed. Cardinal Wolsey founded a grammar school in Ipswich in 1528 that had an even more Renaissance curriculum than St Paul's as it specified that the best Latin was from Classical writers rather than the Church Fathers. These schools would educate the sons of courtiers, gentlemen and merchants and the teaching of Terence, Virgil, Cicero, Horace, Quintilian and Ovid was now compulsory. The thinking behind the new curriculum was that public service required men trained in virtue and good letters, which meant Latin grammar and the ability to write and speak fluently and with elegance. Good Classical literature would also instil piety and morality.

This was a Christian humanism. The Greeks and Romans were seen to have developed an ethical system which anticipated the Christian revelation and this made the study of the Classics acceptable to the Church. Henry VIII was a great supporter of these changes and his family were brought up with a humanist education. But the English take on the humanist Renaissance in Italy was very much a utilitarian one. It would improve and refine the scholastic approach to education rather than replace it. The changes in the education system would produce scholars better equipped for their diplomatic, ecclesiastical or administrative careers, but studying the Classical past as an end in itself, especially the Greek past, would have to wait until the sixteenth and seventeenth centuries.

The immediate effect of the English Reformation was to largely cut off links with Italy so that sharing of scholarship was limited, and being seen to have an interest in Latin was potentially dangerous. But studying the Classics at school and university continued for another 400 years. Edward Thring, the founder of the Headmasters' Conference and Headmaster of Uppingham for twenty years wrote in 1864: *"Let the mind be educated in one noble subject. If this subject also embraces a wide field of knowledge so much the better. The universal consent of many ages has found such a subject in the study of Latin and Greek literature"*.

How important was printing to the success of the Italian Renaissance?

It has been noted that the written inheritance of Western civilisation had been fragmented in courts, monasteries and palaces throughout Europe and beyond in the case of Greek texts. Humanists had been instrumental in recovering many of these texts and re-introducing the knowledge of Greek literature.

Printing, which began in 1455 in Germany, had the task of reproducing these texts and spreading the scholarship of the Renaissance. In 1450, a good library might have 100 manuscript books. By 1550, a single scholar could expect to have 100 printed books. What had once been scarce and fragmented was now available to almost anyone who was literate. Perhaps Lord Acton summed up the contribution best in 1895 when he said: *Print gave assurance that the work of the*

Renaissance would last, that what was written would be accessible to all, that such an occultation of knowledge and ideas as had depressed the Middle Ages would never recur, that not an idea would be lost.

The next two chapters will look at the work of these early printers.

Illustration of a sixteenth century continental printing shop.

VII

THE SCHOLAR PRINTERS

A man born in 1453, the year of the fall of Constantinople, could look back from his fiftieth year on a lifetime in which about eight million books had been printed, more perhaps than all the scribes of Europe had produced since Constantine founded the city in AD330.

Elizabeth Eisenstein (1997)

This chapter will look at some of the great scholar printers. The following chapter will be a more general look at the conditions that they faced, and why they succeeded when many other printers failed. It should be remembered that in this first 100 years of printing, the functions of type-founder, printer, publisher, editor and bookseller were often combined in the one man or his close associates. By the end of the period, type-founding, printing, publishing and bookselling had become established as largely separate occupations.

When did printing begin?

Johannes Gutenberg had experimented with printing by movable metal type in Strasbourg between 1436/9. He then perfected his process in Mainz from 1450/5 culminating in the printing of the

42 line Bible. There must have been experimentation with simple indulgences and calendars before he could produce a book as astonishingly beautiful as this first printed Bible, but nothing survives to tell us how he made progress. Gutenberg had been a goldsmith and so was used to working with metal and could cut the punches used to make the individual sorts or pieces of type. His main invention was to design the adjustable hand moulds for casting type that could permit different widths for the letters of the alphabet, eg the broad letter W and the narrow letter I. He still, however, had to work out the composition of the metal alloy to pour into the moulds with low melting point and quick, undistorted solidification. A new type of ink had to be made that would adhere to metal and yet not smudge and dry quickly when applied to the paper. And a press had to be designed based on the wine presses of the region. (Anyone wanting to know more about the technical process is referred to the reading list, especially Gaskell, 1972).

Gutenberg was an inventor rather than a scholar printer. Shortly after printing the famous 42 line Bible, his financial backer, Fust, took him to court in 1456 for not repaying the loan needed to finance printing the Bible. Having won the case, Fust then took over the printing shop and installed his son-in-law, Peter Schöffer, as the man in charge. Gutenberg may have printed after this in Bamberg before his death in 1468, but there is no real evidence of his future activity.

A number of people had learnt printing from working with Gutenberg. Mainz became a centre for printing until 1462, when the town was sacked in a dispute between rival archbishops. This led to the exodus of skills which can be traced to other cities in Germany as well as to Italy and France and beyond.

Italy

Although divided into states, fifteenth century Italy was the richest and culturally most dynamic region in Europe. Venice in particular held many attractions: it had a tolerance of other cultures and religions; the nobles were rich; many manuscripts were available, especially from Greek scholars who had fled before the fall of Constantinople in 1453; and there was a learned group of lay and ecclesiastic scholars familiar with purchasing books. In addition, the government offered protection to all who settled there and the port offered easy import and export of materials including paper. Venice also had a long history of mercantile and financial predisposition to risk through its sea trading with the Middle East and Asia, and a well developed banking system. Even small investors could buy shares in these trading ventures and so a new technology, where people could see paper turned into a value added commodity after printing, was an attractive investment. And a book industry that would produce far more copies than the local market could absorb needed to export. Venice had the existing distribution network to facilitate this export both by sea and road.

The first printers in Italy were German, Arnold Pannartz and Konrad Sweynheim, both of whom were in holy orders. It is believed that Sweynheim had worked with Gutenberg. They were invited by the Abbot of the Benedictine monastery at Subiaco, sixty miles from Rome, to set up a printing press in 1464. The monks of Subiaco monastery included a number of Germans who had heard about the invention of printing in their native country. Sweynheim and Pannartz printed 4 books there before moving on to the Massimi Palace in Rome in 1467. Even with appeals for the help of Pope Sixtus IV, they could not successfully remain in business and their partnership ended in 1472. By that time they had printed 29 works of Latin classics and works by the Church Fathers in editions of 275 copies of each volume.

The first printer in Venice was also German, Johann von Speyer, who began printing in 1468. He had trained as a goldsmith, like Gutenberg, and was one of the printers forced to leave Mainz in 1462 when the city was sacked. The Collegio of Venice granted Speyer a five year exclusive privilege to print in the city, but he died after only a year and the privilege died with him. This may have been fortunate as a host of other entrepreneurial printers followed him to make Venice the printing capital of the fifteenth century. By 1500, there were 233 printing presses working in Venice at a time when there were only five printers working in London. Some 4,000 editions producing over one million volumes would be printed in Venice, or almost 15% of all incunabula (books printed before 1501). According to Nuovo (2015), nearly half of these editions were printed by Germans.

Nicolas Jenson (1420–80)

Amongst the scholar printers of Venice, Nicolas Jenson is one of the outstanding figures. He was French and was sent in 1458 by Charles VII from his post as Master of the Royal Mint at Tours to Mainz to learn about printing with metal type. (This could be deemed an early incidence of French industrial espionage). It is assumed that when Charles VII died in 1461, Jenson felt that France would not be so receptive to his newly learned skills; and so he moved to Venice instead and started printing there in 1470. Jenson, who was not a scholar but whose printed books were scholarly, contributed his metal working, design skills and entrepreneurial abilities to earn a reputation as the finest printer in Europe.

He was an expert engraver and cut his own punches to make the type. Some have suggested that his earlier work on coins and medals may have given him greater sensitivity to the sculptural nature of type than was natural for the goldsmiths who became punch cutters. It was the grandeur and perfect lay-out of his Latin classics which were admired for their beauty and legibility. His own firm put out a claim in 1482 that *"his books do not hinder one's eyes, but rather help them and do them good. Moreover, the characters are so intelligently and carefully elaborated that the letters are neither smaller, larger nor thicker than reason and pleasure demand"*. In particular it was his roman type based on humanist calligraphy that distinguishes Jenson. William Morris made Jenson's roman type well-known in Victorian times.

Morris used it for the Kelmscott Press, naming it his Golden type. The humanists had largely rejected gothic script as representing the ignorance of scholasticism.

As well as his metal working and design skills, Jenson was essentially a businessman. He printed the Classics but was happy to also print books of law or liturgy if that is what the market wanted. In part this was forced on him as by 1473 there was a glut of unsold Classical books in Venice and printers were forced to cut back supply. He also designed a gothic fount, primarily for his law books, and a Greek type, and rarely used the roman type after 1474 unless commissioned to do so for particular editions.

Jenson produced some 160 editions in his ten years of printing in Venice. Many of these are Roman classics, including the works of Julius Caesar, *Attic Nights* of Aulus Gellius, and the *Historia Naturalis* of Pliny the Elder. His Greek type was mainly used for quotations.

In the later 1470s competition increased. Principally, Jenson was competing with Johannes de Colonia, another German printer, who had married the widow of Johann von Speyer. Because of the additional financial clout of his competitor, Jenson felt he needed to bolster his own finances and Peter Uglheimer, a merchant originally from Frankfurt, went into a partnership with him in order to provide the additional money. Following an outbreak of plague in 1478, the rival firms of Jenson and Johannes de Colonia decided to amalgamate. This partnership was short-lived as both of the printers died in 1480. Shortly before Jenson died, Pope Sixtus IV conferred on him the honorary title of Count Palatinate.

According to Lowry (1969): *Jenson was a pioneer, using a new technology to preserve the past and enlighten the future. His work combined enlightened patronage, literary commitment, artistic genius and technical skill.*

Aldus Manutius (1450-1515)

Aldus came to be a printer/publisher quite late in life. He was 45 when his print shop opened in 1495, by which time there were already 200 other presses operating in Venice. His earlier life was that of a typical humanist, teaching the Classics to aristocratic youths and writing Latin and Greek grammars to help pay the bills. However, his ambition as a humanist was to bring enlightenment through the study of Classical literature which was then known to very few. He was concerned that after the fall of Constantinople to the Turks in 1453, the dispersal of Greek scholars and their libraries would mean the loss of Greek literature. Humanists were well aware of the loss of earlier Classical learning as previous chapters have noted.

To fulfil his ambitions, Aldus saw as his purpose in life the printing of the Classics, especially the Greek classics, both in order to preserve them, and to spread the knowledge of Greek language and culture among fellow humanists . This ambition was born in the 1480s when his studies at Ferrara were interrupted by war between Ferrara and the Venetians. One of his fellow students was the key Renaissance figure of Pico Della Mirandola, author of *Oration on the Dignity of Man*, who invited Aldus to stay with him when hostilities closed the university. During his two year stay with Pico he met Emanuel Adramyttenos, one of the many Greek scholars in exile from Constantinople. Aldus improved his knowledge of Greek language and literature during this period. It also led to him becoming tutor to the sons of Pico's sister who was the Princess of Carpi. At some stage in this part of his life he decided to dedicate himself to printing the Greek classics and it was the financial assistance of the Princess and her sons that enabled him to set up his press in Venice in 1494.

He chose Venice for his printing press because of its pre-eminence in printing and because it was home to thousands of Greek refugees, many with manuscripts or with the skills to assist him as grammarians, typesetters and proofreaders. To this end he printed the texts from ancient manuscripts in 'plain text' with no commentaries or translation.

Whereas Nicolas Jenson had the commercial and technical expertise but relied on others for the scholarly input, Aldus was the opposite. It is probably fairer to describe Aldus as a publisher rather than a printer. Francesco Griffo (1450–1518) was the punch cutter who designed his types; the roman, Greek and italic types were of pure Renaissance inspiration and design. Aldus gave the printed text the academic and social respectability previously enjoyed by the manuscript. By setting the textual standard both for his contemporaries in the trade and for later academic publishers, Aldus' editions contributed greatly to improve the quality of scholarship in all leading universities around Europe. As an example, the two Regius Professors of Greek at Oxford and Cambridge were founded in the 1540s by Henry VIII, in part because of the availability of textual material from Venice.

In 1500, Aldus founded an "academy" of like- minded scholars who acted as editors, readers, correctors and others who could bring influence to bear on his work. Erasmus, for example, lived with Aldus in 1508 acting as a consultant editor. Other members of this Aldine Academy included Marcus Musurus, a professor of Greek who is credited with editing most of the Greek titles. Aldus had first met Musurus during his stay with the Carpis. Musurus is said to have rivalled Erasmus in his learning. Another member was Pietro Bembo who was both a cardinal and literary theorist. (The Bembo type developed in the 1920s is named for him after the 1496 book of his poems published by Aldus). Martin Lowry (1989) says that Aldus' household was an "*almost incredible mixture of the sweat shop, the boarding house and the research institute.*"

It is known that Aldus used some type moulds that had been made originally by Jenson. In 1479, the type moulds were sold to Andrea Torresani by Jenson, with whom he had worked. It came into Aldus' possession when he moved in with Torresani who had become his father-in-law. Torresani was also a source of financial support following the initial assistance from the Carpis. However, the type that made Aldus famous was the italic which was revolutionary. It was smaller and more compact which allowed more text per page and thus saved paper which was a costly element in book production at the time. And eventually, the Aldine Press became best known for its smaller size, octavo, books which were both more portable and affordable for scholars. Aldus called these *libri portatiles* in his promotional flysheets. He was also one of the earliest printers to introduce page numbering.

Aldus was not a natural businessman. Unlike some of the printers discussed below, he had no marketing model beyond relying on personal recommendations and corresponding individually with book buyers. He only appointed agents north of the Alps to take orders at a very late stage and had no presence at the Frankfurt Book Fair. Partly because of this, he suffered greatly from the piracy of his books by printers in Lyons and Cologne.

As he became more famous, he found the correspondence and personal callers time-consuming and irritating. This did, however, lead him to produce in 1498 a priced listing of his publications to use as a short cut and this is believed to be the first priced catalogue ever issued by a publisher. In the year before his death, the distractions from personal callers was such that he put up a notice outside his office saying: *"Whoever thou art, thou art earnestly requested by Aldus to state thy business briefly and to take thy departure promptly. In this way thou mayst be of service even as was Hercules to the weary Atlas. For this is a place of work to all who may enter"*.

Before his death in 1515, Aldus had printed the works of Aristotle, Plato, Homer, Pindar, Euripides, Sophocles, Aristophanes, Demosthenes, Lysias, Herodotus, Thucydides, Plutarch, Dioscorides and Xenophon as well as a series of books by the main Roman writers. In total there were some 100 works which came out in about 250 volumes.

The first major book Aldus published in Greek is the set of five volumes of the works of Aristotle printed between 1495-8. Karl Schottenloher (1989) claimed that this set can be *"designated as the greatest literary and typographical undertaking of the fifteenth century"*. It is interesting that an early English humanist, Thomas Linacre (1460–1524), who had learnt Greek in Italy, helped edit some of this edition. Aldus presented him with a set printed on vellum which Linacre returned with him to New College, Oxford, where it remains in the college library.

At Aldus's funeral, humanists erected a display of all of these books around his coffin. In his birthplace, Bassanio in Italy, a monument erected to him bears his own words, "*I should like to be remembered for the abundance of good books which, we hope, will finally put to flight all ignorance*".

Given the constraints of fifteenth century life, the achievement of securing and evaluating the original manuscripts, preparing the texts for the press and printing them correctly, and coping with all the other difficulties of early printers that we will look at later, Aldus could lay claim to having the greatest and most honourable name in the history of publishing. He did not die a wealthy man, sales were hindered as only some 5% of humanists could read Greek without notes, but his life was rich in accomplishment and the companionship of so many noteworthy people who shared his public spiritedness and scholarly ideals. The Aldine Press continued under his son and grandson until 1597.

Erhard Ratdolt (1442–1528)

Ratdolt was one of the many German printers who moved to Venice. He printed there from 1476–86 before returning to his native Augsburg. In Venice he started work in association with two fellow German printers, Bernhard Maler and Peter Löslein. It would appear that Maler was the boss, Ratdolt the printer, and Löslein the corrector. The first book the firm published was the *Kalendarium* of Regiomontanus in 1476 and this was the first ever book to have a title page.

Ratdolt was one of the most technically ambitious of the early printers and one of the few who printed mathematical and scientific works. He is most famous for his 1482 printing of Euclid's *Elements* which used the Adelard of Bath/Campanus translation from the Greek and Arabic. This book brilliantly solved the technical problems of relating, if not integrating, illustrations to text, and included 420 woodcuts to illustrate Euclid's geometry. Euclid's work had circulated in Europe in manuscript since the twelfth century, but the number of reprints made of the printed copy showed how much demand had been unsatisfied with the earlier technology. This first printing of Euclid completed its 1,800 year journey from papyrus in Alexandria, through its translations into Arabic and then Latin, and finally into a paper book. Ratdolt printed a number of books about astronomy by Arabic scientists.

Ratdolt had also designed a very attractive roman typeface which could rival Jenson's, and many of his books had attractive printed borders; a style that William Morris again copied for the Kelmscott Press. After only two years the partnership with Maler and Löslein ended, but Ratdolt remained in Venice for another eight years. During that time he further innovated by producing a specimen sheet to show the types he could use, and the earliest known publisher's catalogue listing his books for sale, although unpriced.

It has to be conceded that not all Italian printers lived up to these high standards. Pettegree (2010) points out that, as with any new technology, the initial enthusiasm and expansion often has to go through a painful period of adjustment if it has expanded beyond what the market can absorb. This stage was reached in Italy in the early 1470s when so many printed books of the Classics were unsold that eight of the twelve printers in Venice went bankrupt. Some printers had produced books that were dirty, smudged and inaccurate. Many readers felt that this was debasing the book as the standard of manuscript books in Venice had been very high.

Before leaving Italy it is worth noting that **Florence** made almost no contribution to early printing. Given that it was the home of Petrarch, Dante and Boccaccio and the main hub of the Renaissance, this seems especially surprising. A printing press set up in the city in

1471 failed and only in 1474 was another established, and this in a convent. The thinking is that the Florentines had produced the best manuscript books in Italy and held themselves in such high esteem that printed books were regarded as vulgar. Only the local Giunti family succeeded and grew with branches throughout Europe; but they were essentially publishers of textbooks and more popular vernacular titles.

France

The first printers in France were again German. Ulrich Gering, Michael Friburger and Martin Crantz were invited by the Rector of the Sorbonne to set up a press in the university in Paris in 1469. They produced 22 works subsidised by the university between 1470-2 before setting up on their own. Printing took time to reach Paris because of opposition. Strasbourg had a press in 1460, but the estimated 6,000 scribes and illuminators in Paris had already confiscated books brought from Mainz by Fust as they recognised the threat to their livelihoods.

By the second quarter of the sixteenth century, Paris had taken over from Venice as the capital of fine book making, and printed more books than Venice. The physical and intellectual quality of Italian books had declined, partly as commercial decisions were coming before scholarship. Essentially, a new reading public had evolved and they were willing to trade beauty for cheaper books. And the restrictions of the Inquisition reached Venice in 1547. Amongst other restraints, the Inquisition led to a ban on printing in Hebrew from 1554. The decline of major Italian publishing firms also resulted in part from the crisis in the Venetian Republic from 1499-1504; bouts of plague; defeat by the League of Cambrai after the 1508/10 war; strong foreign competition; the shift of the commercial axis of Europe from the Mediterranean to the Atlantic after the Portuguese and Spanish voyages of discovery; and the growing expertise of northern European scholars. All of these factors combined to tip the balance in favour of France.

There were a number of very creative French type designers and punch cutters who were working independently selling their type to major printing houses. Claude Garamond was active from 1520–60 and eventually his roman type was bought by the Aldine Press in Venice to replace the original made by Griffo. Robert Granjon was another type designer becoming of note in the 1550s and later.

The key scholar printers in Paris were Josse Badius and the Estienne family.

Josse Badius (1462-1535) was born in Ghent and a scholar of some repute having studied in Brussels, Louvain, Ferrara and Mantua. He lectured on Roman poets in Paris and Lyons. During his time in Lyons, from 1492/8, he learnt about printing through working as a proof-reader and editor for Johann Trechsel, whose daughter he married. He set up his own press in Paris in 1503 with the help of Jean Petit, one of the university's four accredited booksellers, using first a roman type and then Greek from 1505. Most of his publications, which numbered some 720 works mainly in folio or quarto, were theological and philosophical treatises, grammars and dictionaries, and texts by Classical and humanistic writers. His Classical books, mainly Roman rather than Greek, often carried his own commentaries to make them more approachable for students.

Badius had a close friendship with Erasmus and did more than any other French printer to popularise his work. But in 1517, Erasmus made the decision to have Froben exclusively print his work, largely because Froben had better Greek type. After Badius' death, his printing business merged with that of the Estiennes.

The Estienne family were scholar printers of a similar standing to Aldus Manutius. That said, they were scholars first, and printers second. **Henri Estienne** (1470-1520) was the founder of the dynasty and he started life in the book trade as a bookseller. He began printing by marrying the widow of a German printer who had set up his print shop in Paris in 1484 but died in 1498. Henri printed his first book in 1504 and the Estienne family were printers for 150 years. Henri printed some 100 books, all in Latin.

His second son **Robert Estienne** (1503-1559), who took the Latinised name Robertus Stephanus , became more famous. He was both a Biblical and a Classical scholar and, like Aldus Manutius, wished to focus on printing the Classics. He took over the family business in 1524. His household somewhat resembled Manutius' academy being a collection of intellectuals working as editors and correctors. The household language was Latin which his wife, herself well educated and a daughter of Josse Badius, also spoke. In 1540 he became Royal Printer in Greek to the King, having become Royal Printer in Latin and Hebrew the previous year.

Unfortunately, he was never at ease with the conservative theologians who ran the Sorbonne. They resented his independence and protection from the King and could not reconcile themselves to his correcting texts of the Scriptures and adding marginal commentaries without their permission. They made life so difficult with their attempted censorship of his work that he eventually left Paris in 1552 and set up his printing house in Geneva. There, possibly as a reaction to the Catholic hostility in Paris, he became attracted to the reform ideas of Calvin.

As well as Classical works, he printed humanistic and religious books including a number of versions of the Bible in Greek and Hebrew and introduced the standard numbering of the verses which was universally adopted. His folio printings of Greek classics are especially beautiful.

Robert had three sons who all became printers, one returning to Paris. His exceptional erudition and lifelong dedication to the advancement of learning, combined with his courage in the face of years of bigoted opposition from the university authorities in Paris, mark him out as one of the great scholar printers of the first century of printing.

Switzerland

Basle, because of its location on the borders of France, Germany and Switzerland, had a geographical advantage for the distribution of books at a time when transport was difficult and expensive. Basle was always distinguished by its scholarly printing. The first printer there, Berthold Ruppel, was a pupil of Gutenberg and he set up a press in 1467. But the city's scholarly reputation for printing was established by Johann Amerbach (1443-1513) who had been educated at the Sorbonne. Amerbach learnt his printing as a corrector for Anton Koberger in Nuremberg. He started printing in 1477 and used his press as a vehicle for Christian humanism ensuring his books were printed with great taste and accuracy.

Johann Froben (1460-1527) studied Latin, Greek and Hebrew at the university in Basle. His scholarship was such that, like Aldus Manutius, he was able to prepare for the press a number of texts, including comparison of manuscripts, and correction of typography as well as content. He was trained by Johann Amerbach, twenty years his senior, in typesetting and proof correcting. With his own printing workshop he used a good roman type and was assisted by Hans Holbein in illustrating his work, including the painting of his printer's mark. Holbein was given work as a young man illustrating books for Froben from 1518-1522. It was through Froben recognising his talent that he was recommended to Erasmus, who then secured an invitation from Sir Thomas More for Holbein to visit England, where he stayed and flourished as a court painter for Henry VIII.

In 1516, Desiderius Erasmus chose Froben to print his New Testament in Greek and Latin, one of the key books of the Reformation. Erasmus stayed with Froben at his house quite frequently to oversee publication of his writing and to assist Froben become one of the foremost humanist publishers. Erasmus called him "The Aldus of Germany". Froben was never as prosperous as other publishers who printed works by the Protestant reformers, and he only printed in Latin and Greek. That said, he printed works by Luther from 1518-20, but was then counselled by Erasmus to desist from printing any more.

In his 36 years as a printer, Froben published 257 works, many of them in Greek. He pioneered the sharing of risk in publishing books by collaborating with other printers such as Amerbach and Petri in Basle and Birckmann in Cologne to produce chosen titles.

Froben died after falling from a book ladder. Erasmus was deeply saddened and said that everyone who loved scholarship should wear black. (The Mughal Emperor Humayun met a similar fate in 1556 when he fell down the staircase to his library after hearing the call to prayer. He tried to kneel but his foot caught in his robe, and he died three days later after his head hit stonework on his way down the stairs).

Johann Herwagen (1497-c1558) first printed in Strasbourg from 1523-8, mainly books of the Protestant reformers. He had contacts with Erasmus, who said of him that he was *"a man of good faith and not unlearned"*. A year after Froben died in 1527, he married Froben's widow and so took over the family business. However, in 1531 he set up a printing press in his own name. Scandal broke out in 1538 when he seduced the wife of his stepson, Erasmius Froben, who was also Erasmus' godson. He was brought to trial and fined, but later pardoned. Herwagen mainly printed Roman rather than Greek classics.

Johannes Oporinus (1507-68), whose real surname was Herbst, trained as a proof-reader with Froben. He was a teacher of Latin and Greek in Basle; had a medical degree; and worked with Paracelsus. He then turned to printing full-time. Oporinus was successful and employed fifty workers. He issued three times as many editions as Froben. His publications were quite varied and included a printing of the Qu'ran, which was in Latin, in 1542/3.

As well as classical philology and religious works, he printed the great *De Humani Corporis Fabrica* by the Brussels-born medical professor, Andreas Vesalius, with its superb woodcuts of the human anatomy by Jan van Calcar, a pupil of Titian. The first edition was in 1543. This was one of the great books of the Renaissance, giving doctors a medical textbook based on human dissection unlike the previously accepted work of Galen that was based on dissection of monkeys and pigs. It was a bestseller throughout Europe, superseding all previous Greek and Arabic anatomical texts.

One of the achievements of printing the Greek scientific classics was to enable scientists to read a uniform and correct view of the original work, as far as the accuracy of the manuscripts used by the printers and the quality of the various translations over time had allowed. Printing also aided the reader with contents lists, page numbers, indexes, glossaries and better illustrations. Many manuscript copies would have been hard to find and probably either incomplete or filled with errors. This more widespread dissemination also allowed scientists to assess the failings of works written so long ago, and to improve them with new research that would move science on. It is an interesting coincidence that in 1543 when Vesalius was published, so was the *De Revolutionibus Orbium Coelestium* of Copernicus which gave the heliocentric alternative to Ptolemy's *Almagest*, and *Notable Commentaries on the History of Plants* by the botanist Leonhart Fuchs, which is a herbal with 500 woodcuts, arranged in alphabetical order, that updated Dioscorides.

The role of printing the Greek and Roman classics in the early days of printing should not be exaggerated. Printing certainly ensured that whatever had survived would not be lost again. But only some 5% of the approximately 12 million books printed before 1500 were Classics; and of these, some two thirds were the safe options of Virgil, Cicero, Ovid, Seneca and Terence. These numbers greatly increased in the sixteenth century as printing became more widespread, humanist studies gained greater acceptance in the more traditional universities, and a larger and more educated readership could appreciate them.

VIII

THE BACKGROUND TO
EARLY PRINTING

These volumes, printed in different countries by different printers under untried conditions, seemed to me nothing less than a declaration of independence on the part of a world eager and determined to seek knowledge. No longer was learning to be confined to the fortunate few who could pay the excessive cost of the handwritten volumes, laboriously produced and limited in number; no longer could the wealthy princes presume to hold their political power through the ignorance of the masses. These first printed books, by supplying information concerning spiritual and material things, opened the door to a world until then forbidden, and marked the turning point in history by giving the people a weapon with which to fight against bigotry and oppression. They were not merely examples of the art of printing, but were rather mirrors in which were reflected the true beginnings of modern civilization.

William Dana Orcutt, The Kingdom of Books, 1927

How did the book trade work in the manuscript era?

All books were handwritten before 1455. Until about 1100, most of these manuscript books were produced in religious houses. But as universities came into being in Paris, Bologna, and Oxford in the 1100s, expanding rapidly throughout Europe in the following centuries, demand for books increased. Professional scribes began to make copies of books. The universities had a system whereby their official stationer would hire out approved pages of a set book to be copied, and then check the copy when the original was returned. As well as academics, books were required by the clergy, doctors and lawyers, and schools needed textbooks. Within a short time there was a commercial trade in manuscript books and in the early fifteenth century, bookshops selling new and used manuscript books appeared. Monks would often contract out their book production rather than write the books within the monastery, and by 1300, monastic book production was greatly reduced.

Manuscript books could be written on either animal skin or paper. Buying these books was relatively straightforward. The purchaser asked a scribe directly, or more likely a stationer who outsourced requests to a professional scribe, to make a copy of a book. The only "editorial decisions" would be the writing style, whether parchment or paper, the degree of decoration of the pages, and the type of binding. The breakdown of costs was that the scribe took about 50%, the parchment/paper about 20%, the binding 6%, and then the remainder would be taken up with the "extras" of rubrication and possibly illumination. When completed the book was paid for and delivered, usually with no complications of transport, as it would be a local transaction. In short, the scribe would only need to be literate, have a text from which to copy, a supply of paper or parchment, a pen, and some ink. Risk was non-existent as s/he would be paid on completion.

It is interesting that throughout Europe, the workplace for professional scribes was usually close to or even inside the cathedrals or large churches, even though the scribes were not in holy orders like their monastic predecessors. In London the scribes worked in Paternoster Row, next to St Paul's Cathedral, and the book trade in the printed era continued to be centred in and around the churchyard of St Paul's. There was a steady market for second hand manuscript books, particularly in university towns.

It would be a mistake to think that books were scarce by the mid 1450s. Scribes were meeting demand sometimes on an almost industrial scale as with the production of portable Bibles in Paris in the fourteenth century, and *Books of Hours* in Bruges and other Flemish towns. School pupils were increasingly requiring textbooks. Any town with a university, a cathedral, law courts or government administrative offices would have commercial copying centres where the scribes could be found. And it was this growth in manuscript books that led to the foundation of libraries, ie separate spaces for books rather than locked cupboards and boxes, in the late fourteenth and fifteenth centuries.

What changed with printing?

As noted in the previous chapter, the invention of printing is credited to Gutenberg with 1455 as the start date. The first few years of printing follow a similar pattern to that of any new technology. There was no great vision of where print was going. The first books were simply modelled on existing manuscripts with the intention of producing them more quickly and more cheaply given that the demand for books had been established in the manuscript era. Very early books had type that attempted to replicate the best scribal writing. Spaces were left at the beginning of paragraphs so that rubricators could colour in the initial capitals to make the book more like the manuscript it was replacing. There were few title pages and no page numbers until the 1490s as scribes had not used them. This imitation of manuscripts made some sense in that it was a way of managing the change for buyers who might otherwise have rejected the new product seeing it as vulgar.

What did not make sense was to think that setting up a printing press to replace a copying shop would work commercially. Printed books needed to be produced in large numbers to pay back the initial capital intensive costs of buying the press, type, paper, and the wages of the printers and proof readers. So we see itinerant printers making their way across Europe with their press and type loaded on a mule in search of a patron who was attracted to the prestige of being associated with the new technology and had a few books that s/he wanted reproduced. The German printers Sweynheim and Pannertz moving to the Italian monastery in Subiaco in 1465 is a good example of this early printing phase. There is a long list of noblemen, abbots, bishops and local rulers who hosted a printer for a few years and saw a handful of books printed under their auspices. The failure rate of these early printers was high. Many served prison sentences for debt. Others took to the road to flee their creditors. After printing one or two books for a patron they had to move on, like medieval stonemasons or the early photographers. Harris (2013) notes that printing failed to establish itself in 85% of the Italian towns and cities that had hosted a travelling printer. Buhler (1960) gives a statistic that of the upwards of 350 printers who started a business before 1480, fewer than 10% continued for twenty years.

Most early printers came from humble backgrounds and not a lot is known about them. Buhler (1960) is able to give some analysis of 99 early German printers: 36 had university careers; 22 were artists; 15 belonged to patrician classes; 13 had been scribes; 11 were in holy orders; and 11 had been booksellers or manuscript dealers. But they had to be multi-talented. An early printing press required a master, a journeyman and an apprentice to work it. According to Plant (1965) the master and journeyman had to have *"a good general education, including a knowledge of every dead and living language, perfect accuracy, neatness, quickness of movement, a keen artistic sense, tact and physical strength"*. And that is without considering marketing and distributing their products.

Apart from Gutenberg, who was the true innovator, all printers had learned on the job as has been noted earlier: Froben from working with Amerbach; Badius with Trechsel; Oporinus with Froben; etc. Even Jenson had learned from his time in Mainz but no-one is certain whose workshop he had been attached to. These close connections probably also led to the notable amount of intermarriage between the families as seen by examples in the previous chapter.

Very few even of the later printers became wealthy. Some, like Koberger, had come from affluent backgrounds but the majority of those listed in the previous chapter died as respectable citizens of some distinction, but without amassing a fortune. Economically and socially, successful printers fitted comfortably into the middle-class world of merchants and professionals. They were usually securely above the struggle of lower-class life. But for the many, in these exploratory days, who printed one or two titles before failing for lack of funds or other reasons, going hungry was often the reward for their endeavours.

Why did the early model need consolidation?

By about 1490, it was becoming apparent that the initial enthusiasm by rich patrons for customised print based on the cultural expectations of the manuscript era was not sustainable. Printers needed to have stability, to be self-financing and to be concentrated in major commercial centres rather than satisfying vanity projects in isolated abbeys and princedoms. Books also shook off the need to replicate manuscripts, and so title pages, woodcuts, page numbers and indexes begin to appear in the period of restructuring between 1490 and 1520.

Two principal factors were required for a printer to be successful: a financial sponsor with business sense; and a location that gave both a large local market as well as links to a good distribution network.

Successful printers had **financial backers**. This was because the dominant dilemma of publishing is that it is speculative, unlike the certainty of scribes working on commission. A considerable outlay of capital is required to begin with, whereas turnover can be very slow. Gutenberg relied on the money of Johann Fust, Nicolas Jenson was backed by Uglheimer, Aldus Manutius had Torresano. Johann Fust invested 2,000 gulden into Gutenberg's business. This was a large amount as the Stadtkanzler of Mainz was only earning 208 gulden a year so that we are talking of ten years salary for a senior state official. The money was used to buy 6 presses (about 600 gulden), the vellum for the 35 copies on skin (335 gulden) and the paper for the other approximately 150 copies (at least 500 gulden).

Location was also important for success. It was not just the Church but the intellectual impetus and economic power of the laity who provided the demand for books. That meant it was locating to centres of banking, commerce, industry and trade, with their attendant law courts and universities, that enabled printers to find the regular and required output of work and sales to stay in business. Hence the cities of Venice, Paris, Lyons, Basle, and later Antwerp, became the principal centres of the new technology. The main exception to this was Wittenberg which flourished on printing Martin Luther's work.

Privileges Having invested a large amount of money, intellectual endeavour, risk and labour in printing a new title, publishers wanted protection from having it copied. They needed to sell a large number of copies to recoup their costs. The idea of competition was new to the book trade as the era of manuscript books involved single copies made to order. Copyright as we know it was not introduced until 1709. The system that began in Italy was to grant the publisher a "privilege" for usually five years which prevented anyone else copying or printing the same title. Punishments for transgressors could be severe with stock confiscated and payment of large fines. The problem was that the privilege usually only covered a specific territory so that printers in other parts of the country or overseas had no fear of punishment if they reproduced the book. Certain cities became infamous for book "piracy", especially Lyons. A well known case is the printer Baldassare da Gabiano who tooled himself to make copies of Aldus Manutius' pocket editions. When Aldus learned about this and saw some of the reproductions he was incensed, denouncing them as incorrect. He complained that the paper was bad and had an unusual smell, and sent a long list of corrections to show people in Lyons the error of buying pirated copies. Unfortunately, this just gave Baldassare the authoritative information to make corrections for the next reprint.

Another example of the severity of the problem of book piracy is that of Luther's New Testament first printed in 1522 in an edition of 5,000 that sold out in few weeks. 14 authorised and 66 pirated editions came out in the next two years. And of his complete Bible in German that first appeared in 1534, there were 400 editions in Luther's lifetime, but only a quarter were genuine Wittenberg printings.

What role did marketing have?

The editorial decision of getting right **what to print** was also a major factor in success or failure. Most played safe and printed what had sold well as manuscript books: the Church Fathers, Bibles, liturgical books, law books, school texts, the newly created demand for Greek and Roman classics, but with a good proportion of literature, often in the vernacular. In this first century of printing the only best selling new authors were Erasmus and Luther. Living authors were rarely, if ever, paid any money for their work, printers often being on the breadline. The usual payment was to give the author an agreed number of copies of the finished book, which neatly transferred from the printer the risk of selling them. Such a barter arrangement was very much in favour of the printer as the author usually had to request him to dispose of his copies.

Another of the strategic decisions was **language**: whether to print in Latin/Greek/Hebrew or in the vernacular. The scholar printers all chose Classical or Biblical languages, sometimes, as with Aldus, because they had a humanistic mission which they would put above commercial gain. Printers like Koberger or Froben chose Latin as they could see a European market open to them to justify larger print runs. Others, like Caxton in England, chose vernacular as it represented a niche market that they could successfully compete in. And John Day chose to print in English in support of the Protestant Reformation which largely rejected the Latin of Catholicism. The predominant language throughout Europe for printed books was Latin and this remained so until the mid-seventeenth century. It was only in England and Spain that vernacular printing dominated from the beginning.

Knowing **how many copies to print** was really the make or break decision. Printing too many might mean slow sales and a cash flow problem without the buffer of a rich patron. Worse was to not sell enough to break even, meaning a loss and incurring of debt to suppliers of paper, landlord, workmen, and other stakeholders. On the other hand, printing too few and then having to reset type and print again was inefficient and expensive.

In the early period until the 1480 and 90s, an average print run would be as small as 200 copies moving to 500 by 1500. (There were some exceptions such as law books that the Italian printer Baptista de Tortis could print in editions of 2,300 even before 1500). In the first half of the sixteenth century, editions had moved to between 1,000 and 1,500 and continued in this range for some time. Even Christopher Plantin in Antwerp, who became famous after 1550, kept editions between 1,250 and 1,500. The reasons for the expansion of print runs were the lower costs as books were getting smaller; the market had developed more readers; and distribution had improved. However, it should be remembered that both private and institutional libraries were still small even at the end of this period. Private libraries belonged almost exclusively to lawyers and the clergy. The stock of a university college or cathedral library would be numbered in hundreds of books, and very few private libraries would exceed 1,000 volumes.

Distribution was another key to success. Having produced the books, publishers had to find ways of making potential purchasers aware of what was available and develop a distribution network to supply them. Manuscript makers had not had to think in this way and the printed book was essentially a new product. Printers began producing lists of their publications at quite an early stage, even the 1460s, and these were often put up for display as well as circulated to potential buyers. Full publishers' catalogues became more of a feature of the trade in the 1540s and 1550s.

It was very unlikely that a publisher could sell all the copies printed in his home town or city. But knowing how to sell in other locations, even overseas, was not an easy skill to learn. And then there was the problem of transport and receiving payment. In the earliest days, many printer/publishers would sell directly from their print shop or from a lock-up shop close by as with the market in St Paul's churchyard in London. In large cities such as London and Venice this worked fairly well as customers were able to find the bookshops. But printing in somewhere like Nuremberg meant that Koberger had to choose between finding agents, opening branches, selling on commission or sale-or-return through booksellers in other European countries. Different publishers chose different methods. Italians tended towards having a family member sent to another city to open a branch so that there was close and trusted control. The Giunti family from Florence sent Giacomo to Lyons and he eventually began to print there as well as sell the family's publications. In addition, he was close to another market and could buy French and German books for export to Italy to sell through the family network. Northern European printers favoured having agents.

The role of **transport** was another marketing factor. As the industry became more mature in the 1470s and 1480s, existing merchants who dealt with other goods began to take an interest in printed books. Girolamo Strozzi, a prominent merchant banker in Venice, helped finance some of Nicolas Jenson's publications and he sent these books with other merchandise on his galleys to

Bruges and London. Such a sales strategy for books alone would have been too costly, but using existing transnational commerce routes made it viable.

It must be remembered that books were transported unbound to cut costs: early printed books were usually bound in wooden covers. Transport was expensive and carrying the additional weight of the wooden bindings made no sense when they could be added locally and to the specific tastes of the customer. Books were usually despatched in barrels, wooden trunks or bales wrapped with waxed cotton cloth. Water damage was a major hazard, either from river or sea water when carried by boat, or rain water seeping through covers on ox wagons. Consignments arriving water damaged would not be wasted but often bound and sold at half price.

These hazards were multiplied when consignments needed to be transferred from one vehicle to another. For example, a consignment from Lyons bound for Spain would travel by road as far as the River Loire; then by river to Nantes; then by sea to Spain; to continue by road to Medina del Campo (near Valladolid) which was the distribution centre on account of its fairs.

Once consignments reached their destination satisfactorily, the next problem was **payment**. Sending hard cash via a messenger was unwise given the lawless state of many roads with robbers and stray mercenaries willing to relieve you of your cash. So barter and the bill of exchange were the standard methods of payment. Barter could work where people were willing to exchange stock, and it worked well within Germany. However, often one publisher might feel he was obliged to take stock that was not what he ideally wanted. Dutch printers felt their books were superior to the German ones so that deals had to be done whereby one Dutch book might be exchanged for three German books. The bill of exchange was simpler in that a letter instructing the printer/bookseller's agent/bank in another city to make the appropriate payment was sent, thus avoiding the problem of cash transfer.

Book fairs have always been an important feature in the calendar for anyone connected with the book trade and remain so today. The big international fairs during the period we are looking at were in Lyons and Frankfurt. Publishers would bring books to sell. They would also look at what the competition was doing; listen to authors making a pitch to find a publisher; pay and receive money or make barter arrangements with their agents or wholesalers; meet the book buyers to gain ideas and feedback; and negotiate with any translators looking to select works to extend sales into the vernacular. Most big publishers established warehouses at the fair sites. As an added incentive, many privileges were granted reducing inspection of goods and credentials of foreigners, money lending was permitted, and even convoys of wagons would be escorted. The Frankfurt Book Fair, which was held twice a year, was established very soon after 1455 when Gutenberg first printed. The Lyons fair started soon after and was particularly important for the Italian book trade, having the advantage of being held four times a year.

To give an idea of the scale of sales at book fairs, Christopher Froschauer from Zurich took 2,000 copies of a single title to Frankfurt in 1534. He sold half of them and expected to sell the remainder from his warehouse there in the following fair. Publishers' catalogues were circulated at the fair but the first complete catalogue of all the books at each Frankfurt fair came from an Augsburg bookseller in 1564, and this became one of the main bibliographic tools of the trade for many years.

Book shops became part of the retail scene in most towns and cities. They were sometimes owned by and sold only the publications of a particular printer. But this model meant paying a salary to the manager who often yearned to be able to deal with the books from other sources. It worked best when managed by a family member sent from the printer's home town. Most ordinary people came across printed material such as pamphlets or chap-books being sold either by street sellers in the market square or itinerants on the road carrying baskets of books.

The book shops of the fifteenth and sixteenth centuries looked very different from their counterparts today. They would display not books but loose sheets in packets bearing the author and title of the unbound book. Later, more books would be bound in readiness for sale once the booksellers felt confident of likely customer demand. What booksellers then had in common with counterparts today is that they would strive to have the maximum variety of titles in their stock, often with just one or two copies, rather than stock multiple copies of a smaller range of titles. Shop inventories of the 1480s in Italy indicate a range of size but many shops could offer 1,000 titles even at this early stage of printing. Stock was often arranged in subject order from Classics, religion, law, vernacular works (usually literature), medicine, philosophy, with smaller sections for grammar and children's books.

Book shops were meeting places for the local intelligentsia and became informal local literary societies. New books were displayed for comment and discussion. Unlike academies or courts, book shops were open to all and often allowed younger aspiring literary figures to meet the great and the good of local society. Proprietors were generous in allowing people to come and read their stock even though they had no intention of making a purchase.

By around 1490, a good sales organisation for printers was in place across the whole of Europe.

Why did print succeed?

The aristocracy were not enthusiastic at first. They not only preferred their sumptuous manuscripts but rather resented that their privileged access to the world of learning was now available to people of more moderate standing. But, at first, the Catholic Church welcomed printing with many monasteries and bishops hosting printing presses. One response in Cologne on seeing the first printed books was: *"What an ascent towards God! What ecstatic devotion must we feel on reading the many books printing has given us!"*

whilst another was *"Printing, lately invented in Mainz, is the art of art, the science of sciences. Thanks to its rapid spread the world is endowed with a treasure house of wisdom and knowledge, till now hidden from view. An infinite number of works which very few students could have consulted in Paris or Athens or in the libraries of other great university towns, are now translated into all languages and scattered abroad among all the nations of the earth."*

Despite the mixed reception, certain factors militated in favour of the new invention. **Cost** would become one of the determining factors. Bishop John of Aleria writing to Pope Sixtus IV in 1467 says that it is now possible to buy in Rome for 20 gulden books which a few years earlier would have cost 100. In 1462 Fust brought to Paris the Gutenberg Bible and sold copies for 50 crowns and noted that a manuscript of similar dimension would have cost 400 or 500 crowns. So we know that printed books reduced book prices by at least 80% shortly after they were introduced.

Linked to cost is the increased **quantity** of books that encouraged literacy and education and a greater participation of ordinary people in matters of the day. As Daniel Defoe said, *"The preaching of sermons is talking to a few of mankind, printing books is talking to the whole world"*. Needless to say, various power structures were often threatened by this new inclusivity and so books were banned and burned as were their authors and printers in the period we are examining. It is remarkable how effective repression was despite the numbers of printed books produced. It seems odd that today only two complete copies of Tyndale's 1526 translation of the New Testament into English remain from a print run of 3,000, whereas there are over 250 manuscripts surviving of Wyclif's Bible that were written before 1400.

The **speed** with which books could be printed compared with manuscript production was another major factor. An efficient printing press in this period could produce 2,500 single sided sheets in a day. A scribe might produce 25. The impact of this is clearly seen with Martin Luther and the Reformation in Germany. When he nailed the 95 theses to the church in Wittenberg in October 1517, copies were printed and distributed throughout Germany within two weeks. They had spread to all of Europe within a month. This seems ridiculously slow to us living in the electronic age, but it should be remembered that the break between communication and transport was only made for the first time in 1835 when the telegraph began operating.

Although printing was only an agent of the Protestant Reformation, it was key to its success. Between 1517 and 1520, 400,000 copies of Luther's pamphlets had spread throughout Germany. Luther's criticisms of the Catholic church had been made before by John Wyclif (?1320-1384) and Jan Hus (?1369-1415). But both of these men lived in a manuscript age when copying their work was slow and the numbers of copies vastly smaller, so that the authorities were able to more easily suppress and destroy them to limit the heresy.

Printed books from a scholar printer also had an **authority** that manuscripts were seen to lack. It was assumed that the scholar printer had carefully chosen the most reliable manuscript on which to base his book and that the editors and proof readers would have ensured there were no inaccuracies. Robert Estienne displayed page proofs outside his print shop offering money to anyone who could spot an error. Many printers valued feedback from a first edition so that readers making corrections and criticisms might see them incorporated in a later edition and sometimes with an acknowledgement. This never happened with manuscript books which usually became more inaccurate the more they were copied. Most manuscript books were suspect in that they may have been made from an incomplete or inaccurate manuscript and the scribe could also have made further mistakes in the copying. Manuscript books overseen by universities under the pecia, or approved copying scheme, would be exempt from such criticism.

So it was that many libraries would throw out manuscript books and replace them when a reliable printed copy of the same text arrived. (Audio cassettes and videotapes suffered the same fate in our own time). We also know that the scribe, Peter Meghen, who was scribe to Henry VIII, would only make copies from printed books as he regarded them as more reliable.

Printers would usually distinguish their books with an elaborate woodcut illustration on the title page or the last page. These were effectively trademarks. The use of such a mark, or device, was primarily to defend the scholar printer by protecting him from competition, usually in the form of piracy. But they also enabled the consumer to place trust in a product bearing the mark. Whilst it was not difficult for another printer to copy the text and make a pirate copy of a book, it was harder to forge the woodcuts used to print the mark.

Linked to authority is the **standardisation** that print achieved, especially in relation to scientific data and diagrams. For the first time, identical images, maps, diagrams, mathematical and astronomical tables could be viewed simultaneously by others scattered throughout Europe and beyond. Scribes could not achieve the accuracy of scientific diagrams on a repeated basis whereas an accurate woodcut on a printing press allowed medical and scientific information to be reliably disseminated. Printing also contributed to standardising national languages as the printers normally had to choose the predominant dialect.

Despite these obvious advantages, printed books had a mixed reception. Scribes did not go out of business as print and manuscript co-existed for a considerable time. Some people could afford to buy books in manuscript as they preferred the look and feel of them. Manuscript books were regarded as more intimate and also had an aura of forbidden knowledge. Some authors preferred to control the circulation of their writing which could be done better with hand written and distributed books. And the fifteenth and sixteenth centuries were dangerous times. Many religious and political writings could easily fall foul of the authorities and so printers may well refuse to publish books that could cause them to be fined or worse. We only have to remember in recent times the *samizdat* circulation of hand-written works by dissident authors such as Solzhenitsyn in Soviet Russia to realise the fear of repression.

Summary

In this early phase of printing, many of the scholar printers were achieving their aim of preserving the past in a new and different way. Whereas many ancient texts had survived often because an interested scholar had acted as his own scribe and made a single copy, the humanist printers believed that multiplying the number of copies would prevent the losses of learning from the past ever happening again.

The technical prowess; entrepreneurial flair; ability to attract financial backers; scholarly knowledge and literary judgement; marketing awareness; diplomatic skills to placate officialdom and seek their lucrative contracts; and managerial competence in managing the cash flow, paper and ink supplies and labour in a printing shop, while following complex production schedules; was a set of skills that the most accomplished scribe had never been called on to display. What is even more impressive is that many of the scholar printers had to combine all of these skills themselves, and yet they still produced extraordinarily beautiful books in quite primitive conditions.

The best tribute to them that I have found is in John Addington Symonds *Renaissance in Italy* published in 1875/6:

"The text and the canon of Homer, Plato, Aristotle and the tragedians had to be decided. Greek type had to be struck. Florence, Venice, Basel and Paris groaned with printing presses. The Aldi, the Stephani, and Froben toiled by night and day, employing scores of scholars, men of supreme devotion and of mighty brain, whose work it was to ascertain the right reading of sentences, to accentuate, to punctuate, to commit to the press, and to place

beyond the reach of monkish hatred or envious time, that everlasting solace of humanity which exists in the Classics. All the subsequent achievements in the field of scholarship sink into insignificance beside the labours of these men, who needed genius, enthusiasm, and the sympathy of Europe for the accomplishment of their titanic task. Virgil was printed in 1470, Homer in 1488, Aristotle in 1498, Plato in 1512. They then became the inalienable heritage of mankind. But what vigils, what anxious expenditure of thought, what agonies of doubt and expectation, were endured by those heroes of humanising scholarship. Which of us now warms and thrills with emotion at hearing the name of Aldus Manutius, or of Henricus Stephanus, or of Johannes Froben? Yet, this we surely ought to do; for to them we owe in a great measure the freedom of our spirit, our stores of intellectual enjoyment, our command of the past, our certainty of the future of human culture."

The Prelum Ascensiarum (The press of Ascensius) of Jodocus Badius c1508

Don Carlos de Viana (1421-61) by Jose Moreno Carbonero (1881).

Further reading and list of books consulted

AL-KHALILI, Jim *The House of Wisdom* **Penguin, 2012**

BAEZ, Fernando *A Universal History of the Destruction of Books*
Atlas, 2008

BLAIR, Ann *Too Much to Know: managing scholarly information before the
Modern Age* **Yale UP, 2010**

BOARDMAN, John, etc. *The Oxford History of the Classical World*
OUP, 1986

BROWN, Peter *The World of Late Antiquity: AD150-750*
Thames & Hudson, 1971

BUHLER, Curt *The Fifteenth Century Book*
U. Pennsylvania Press, 1960

CASSON, Lionel *Libraries in the Ancient World* **Yale UP, 2001**

CAVALLO, G. and CHARTIER, R. *A History of Reading in the West*
Polity, 1999

CLAIR, Colin *A History of European Printing* **Academic Press, 1976**

DAVIS, Robert and LINDSMITH, Beth *Renaissance People*
Paul Getty Museum, 2011

EISENSTEIN, Elizabeth *The Printing Revolution in Early Modern Europe* **CUP, 1997**

FEBVRE, Lucien and MARTIN, Henri-Jean *The Coming of the Book* **Verso, 1997**

FISCHER, Steven *A History of Reading* **Reaktion, 2003**

FLANDERS, Judith *A Place for Everything: the curious history of alphabetical order* **Picador, 2020**

FLETCHER, Richard *Moorish Spain* **Phoenix, 2001**

FREELY, John *The Flame of Miletus* **Tauris, 2012**

GASKELL, Philip *A New Introduction to Bibliography* **OUP, 1972**

GRAHAM, Hugh *The Early Irish Monastic Schools: a study of Ireland's contribution to early Medieval culture* **Talbot Press, 1923**

GREENBLATT, Stephen *The Swerve: how the world became modern* **Norton, 2011**

HARRIS, Neil *History of the Book in Italy* **(Chapter 30 in Suarez and Woudhuysen as below)**

HASKINS, Charles Homer *The Renaissance of the Twelfth Century* **Harvard, 1927**

HAY, Denys *The Italian Renaissance in its historical background* **CUP, 1977**

HEALY, John *(Introduction to) Pliny the Elder Natural History: a selection* **Penguin, 2004**

IRWIN, Raymond *The Heritage of the English Library* **Allen & Unwin, 1964**

KARABELL, Z. *People of the Book: forgotten history of Islam and the West* **John Murray, 2007**

KENYON, Frederic *Books and Readers in Ancient Greece and Rome* **OUP, 1932**

KILGOUR, Frederick *The Evolution of the Book* **OUP, 1998**

KONIG, Jason (ed.) *Ancient Libraries* **CUP, 2013**

LERNER, Fred *The Story of Libraries* **Continuum, 1999**

LINDBERG, David *The Beginnings of Western Science: Prehistory to 1450* **U. Chicago Press, 2007**

LOWRY, Martin *Venetian Printing* **Poul Kristensen, 1989**

MACLEOD, Roy *The Library of Alexandria* **Tauris, 2000**

McNEELY, Ian and WOLVERTON, Lisa *Reinventing Knowledge; from Alexandria to the Internet* **Norton, 2009**

MANGUEL, Alberto *A History of Reading* **Harper Collins, 1996**

MOLLER, Violet *The Map of Knowledge: how Classical ideas were lost and found* **Picador, 2019**

NUOVO, Angela *The Book Trade in the Italian Renaissance* **Brill, 2013**

O'LEARY, De Lacy *How Greek Science passed to the Arabs* **Routledge, 1948**

PETTEGREE, Andrew *The Book in the Renaissance* **Yale UP, 2010**

PINNER, H. L. *The World of Books in Classical Antiquity* **Sijthoff (Leiden), 1948**

PLANT, Marjorie *The English Book Trade* **Allen & Unwin, 1965**

PRESTWICH, Michael *Medieval People* **Thames and Hudson, 2014**

PUTNAM, George *Authors and Their Public in Ancient Times* **Cooper Square, 1967**

REYNOLDS, L. D. and WILSON, N. G. *Scribes and Scholars: a guide to the transmission of Greek and Latin literature* **Clarendon, 1968**

SAVAGE, E. A. *Old English Libraries* **Methuen, 1911**

SCHLOTTENLOHER, Karl *Books and the Western World*
McFarland, 1989

STAIKOS, Konstantinos *Libraries From Antiquity to the Renaissance*
Basil, 1997

STEINBERG, S. H. *Five Hundred Years of Printing* **British Library, 1996**

STRONG, Roy *The Spirit of Britain* **Hutchinson, 1999**

SUAREZ, Michael and WOUDHUYSEN, H. R. *The Book: a global history* **OUP, 2013**

THOMPSON, James Westfall *The Medieval Library* **Hafner, 1957**

WATT, W. Montgomery *The Influence of Islam on Medieval Europe*
U. Edinburgh P., 1972

WEISS, R. *Humanism in England in the Fifteenth Century* **Blackwell, 1951**

WEST, Andrew *Alcuin and the Rise of Christian Schools*
Scribners, 1892

WHITFIELD, Peter *Landmarks in Western Science*
British Library, 1999

WINSBURY, Rex *The Roman Book* **Bristol Classical Press, 2009**

WORMALD, F. & WRIGHT, C.E. *The English Library Before 1700* **U. London P., 1958**

ZIMMER, H. *The Irish Element in Mediaeval Culture* **Putnam, 1891**

and various episodes from the BBC Radio 4's *In our time* archive provide excellent introductions.

Index

A